# LANDSCAPE
## MAGIC

# LANDSCAPE MAGIC

## Tricks & Techniques
## for Rejuvenating Old Yards & Gardens

### DOUGLAS GREEN

PHOTOGRAPHY BY RICHARD W. BROWN

ILLUSTRATIONS BY VINCE BABAK

CHAPTERS PUBLISHING, LTD., SHELBURNE, VERMONT 05482

Published by
Chapters Publishing Ltd.
2031 Shelburne Road
Shelburne, Vermont 05482

**Library of Congress Cataloging-in-Publication Data**

Green, Douglas.
    Landscape Magic: tricks & techniques for rejuvenating old yards & gardens /
by Douglas Green; illustrations by Vince Babak.
        p.      cm.
    Includes bibliographical references (p.  ) and index.
    ISBN 1-881527-86-7 (hardcover). — ISBN 1-881527-85-9 (paperback)
    1. Gardening. 2. Landscape gardening.  I. Title.
SB453.G78  1995
635—dc20                                                            95-22369

Trade distribution in Canada by
Firefly Books Ltd.
250 Sparks Avenue
Willowdale, Ontario
Canada M2H 2S4

Trade distribution in the U.S. by
Firefly Books (U.S.) Inc.
P.O. Box 1338
Ellicott Station
Buffalo, NY  14205

Printed and bound in Canada by Metropole Litho, Inc.
St. Bruno de Montarville, Quebec

Cover design by Susan McClellan
Cover photograph by Richard W. Brown
Inside design by Eugenie Seidenberg Delaney and Susan McClellan

*For Christie*

*For your questions*
*For your wandering dreams.*

# ACKNOWLEDGMENTS

W RITING A BOOK has been very much like growing plants in our nursery business. Both activities show the results of germination, loving care, hard work and pruning before becoming useful in the garden. While I tend to get the praise for both the plants and the book, I have to confess that I don't do all the work. Many people have contributed to this book right from the earliest stages. While I accept the praise if the book helps and the blame for any errors, these people deserve mention for their unique roles:

Andrea, for teaching me about flow, and for being there from the germination to the final harvest.

My children, Christie, Jennie, Robbie and Elizabeth, for doing all the weeding while I was doing the typing and for not complaining about it to my face.

Susan Urstadt, my agent, who knows where we started, what we accomplished and how much I appreciate her help.

Barry, Alice and Paul, at Chapters Publishing, who discovered what April and May mean in the nursery business and who still talk to me in spite of it.

Denise Bowes and Carol Pratt for their unique viewpoints on how a garden book should talk to readers.

My customers and friends who asked the questions and told me to put the answers in a book.

# CONTENTS

# INTRODUCTION

*"Oh, Adam was a gardener, and God who made him sees*
*That half a proper gardener's work is done upon his knees,*
*So when your work is finished, you can wash your hands and pray*
*For the Glory of the Garden, that it may never pass away."*

J.R. KIPLING (1865-1936)
***The Glory of the Garden***

I N A DELIGHTFUL BOOK CALLED *The Secret Garden*, written more than 80 years ago by Frances Hodgson Burnett, a little girl, orphaned and lonely on her uncle's great estate on the moors of England, discovers a neglected garden, enclosed behind a brick wall and a locked door. She shares her discovery with her cousin, a sickly and imperious young boy, and with a robust moorland lad whose knowledge of plants is instinctive and inspiring. Together the children clandestinely restore the landscape. As they weed, prune and nurture the plants back to their former beauty, the children themselves grow and heal.

Burnett's story speaks to any one of us who has confronted an overgrown landscape or struggled to stay a few steps ahead of the relentless weeds. The sight of roses climbing aimlessly or flowering shrubs gone ragged from neglect can be discouraging, and tackling these projects may at first seem overwhelming, but once begun, the task of restoration becomes its own reward.

"Where do I start?" and "What do I do with all of this?" are among the most common questions we hear at our nursery, especially from people who have just bought a house and find themselves overwhelmed by the former owner's horticultural legacy. This book provides some answers. Like Dickon, the moorland lad, it is intended to be instructive and inspirational. It offers guidance to homeowners, and it provides a comforting prescription to anyone who has caught a touch of "catalogue fever" and has seemingly ordered one of everything in the book and is now struggling to keep up. Even experienced gardeners can learn a number of techniques to enhance their efforts. Every reader, I hope, will acquire the skills to bring order to chaos or renewed vigor to mature plantings.

Each chapter focuses on a specific range of plants or gardening conditions. The work of renewal and maintenance is broken down into easily accomplished tasks. Approached one step at a time, garden renovation steadily produces more visible and satisfying results.

*Azaleas add a splash of vibrant red to this shady garden.*

Twenty years of gardening and nursery experience make this a practical book, gleaned from the bare-knuckle, down-in-the-dirt school of education. I am as proud of the dirt under my nails and the stains in the cracks of my fingers as I am of any graduate degree.

Over the years, misinformation has slipped into gardening literature and has been passed on from generation to generation. At times, I take issue with this "conventional wisdom." What I recount here is my own understanding of how plants grow and what they need to flourish. I explain each step as I have accomplished it in my own garden.

Even as a professional, surrounded by thousands of plants on a daily basis, I am constantly reminded of the magic and glory of the garden. In the midst of a hectic spring, working from dawn to nightfall, I still marvel at the newly emerging bulbs and germinating seeds. I find excitement in the first geranium blossom and the earliest perennial to poke its head up after a long, hard winter.

There is a balance in gardening between work and delight, fatigue and relaxation, frustration and accomplishment. This balance keeps us humble, knowing that there is always more to learn from this glory we call a garden. Gardens are places to rest and reflect as well as to labor, and without some comfortable place to sit, the only time spent in the garden will be time spent working. Work, it's true, benefits the body and lifts the spirits, but taking a moment's rest—enjoying the beauty of the flowers or the full promise of the vegetables—is food for the soul. I believe, like Kipling, that washing your hands at the end of a satisfying stretch of gardening and looking over your handiwork is a delight you can only hope "will never pass away."

# CHAPTER ONE

# *A*NNUAL FLOWER GARDENS

*"There's a flower that shall be mine,
'Tis the little celandine"*

WILLIAM WORDSWORTH (1770-1850)
*To the Small Celandine*

A NNUAL FLOWERS BLOOM FOR ALL OR PART OF THE summer before exhausting themselves or succumbing to the ravages of heavy frost and winter cold. Annuals are plants that can complete their life cycle—from germination to flowering to seed production—in a single season, unlike biennials, which grow and produce seed on a two-year cycle, or perennials, which return season after season. Some annuals can be put in pots and carried inside and nurtured through the winter to provide cuttings for next spring's garden, but for the most part, annuals are a one-season phenomenon. Annuals offer gardeners an incredible choice of colors, shapes and heights. At our nursery, we raise more than 500 distinct varieties. Like the versatile flowers themselves, any planting arrangement and color scheme lasts only a year. It may seem strange to discuss renovating plants that, for the most part, are with us for only one season, but there are many things a gardener can do to increase the vigor of annuals and the abundance of their flowers.

*Attentive care can increase the vigor of annual flowers, such as these poppies.*

# PRUNING FOR NEW GROWTH

THE SINGLE MOST IMPORTANT CONCEPT OF renovation is that pruning stimulates new growth. The harder you prune, the more new growth a plant will generate. There is obviously a point of no return, but as long as a plant has healthy leaves, new growth will spring from dormant buds along the length of the remaining stems. Annuals can be pruned in one of two ways: nonselectively or selectively.

## NONSELECTIVE PRUNING

In nonselective pruning, the gardener simply gives annuals a level haircut. Hedge shears work well for this kind of renovation, because you can easily make large cuts on tender stems with this tool. Under ideal conditions, annuals will begin to bloom vigorously again two to three weeks after a drastic shearing (when the plant height is reduced by up to one-half).

Petunias and other plants in hanging baskets often get leggy as the summer progresses, and they respond to shearing with increased foliage and new bulk. Plants that flower on new wood, such as fuchsia, will respond to a general shearing with a great deal of new wood and a resulting flush of flowers. However, fuchsias and other woody-stemmed plants take much longer to come back into bloom than softer-stemmed annuals, such as petunias, impatiens and geraniums.

Plants that have been overwintered in the house benefit from a nonselective pruning before they are returned to the garden in the spring. Drastic pruning forces the plant to start new, compact shoots that will look better than the thin, watery, pale growth produced in the back bedroom over the winter. Geraniums, for example, look leggy after a winter of low sunlight levels, but if they are cut back to 8 to 12 inches, fed well with a liquid plant food and exposed to as much sunlight as possible, they will respond by producing many new shoots. If indoor gardeners time their renovation to coincide with the increasing sunlight levels toward the middle of March, the plants will respond dramatically

and will flower prolifically all summer on new growth. You can also generate dozens of new plants by pruning—put the severed shoots in a glass of water and transplant them after they sprout roots.

I remember well the first time I ever saw anyone shear a geranium. An old gardener named Mr. Tuttle brought a magnificent 3-foot-tall blooming geranium into a class from his greenhouse. In a wonderful lecture on how to propagate geraniums, he began to dismember the plant before our eyes. He gradually snipped it here and there to produce perfectly even 3-inch cuttings for propagation. Once the tender shoots had been harvested, the work began in earnest and branch after branch was ruthlessly cut. Only his twinkling eyes and a twitch of his mouth betrayed his amusement as he watched the faces of innocent students observing what could only be described as plant slaughter. The poor plant was left with only a few straggly leaves and 12 inches of old stalks sticking out from the pot at odd angles. A month later, Mr. Tuttle brought the geranium back. It still had no flowers, but it was covered with lush new growth.

On plants that are just beginning to stretch, a less drastic shearing—taking only 1 inch of stem—will very quickly produce new growth. If the plant is straggly, removing more than an inch of growth will help restore it to display condition.

## SELECTIVE PRUNING

Nonselective pruning is the approach most gardeners take when they are raising large beds of soft-stemmed annuals, since there is rarely time to design each plant's specific shape. However, trimming plants individually can prevent the need for a nonselective leveling. In selective pruning, specific leading growth stems are removed in order to control and shape plant growth. As soon as the growing tip is removed, side shoots begin to burst from leaf axils farther down the stem. (Axils are the joints where the leaf emerges from the stem.)

Gardeners refer to removing a lot of stem as a "hard pinch" and a small amount as a "soft pinch." The

## SELECTIVE PRUNING OF ANNUALS

*Cutting back specific stems enables a gardener to control and shape plant growth.*

It is almost impossible to kill an annual by pruning. They recover quickly from all but the most severe trim. Experiment with various styles and degrees of pruning. You will quickly see how different annuals respond to your attention, and what you will learn is well worth the price of a few packs of seed.

Cutting or breaking off dead flowers might be considered a type of pruning. Although tedious, deadheading is an important part of plant care. It not only enhances the appearance of a plant, but it can also improve the plant's health. Dead flowers are prime hosts for diseases, so when you remove these flowers, you reduce the incidence of many fungal ailments. Deadheading also encourages some annuals, such as salvia, to continue blooming. Annuals are genetically programmed to produce seed. If the gardener removes spent blooms in which the seeds would normally mature, the plant will respond with another flower.

Precisely where to remove blossoms is a decision that has to be made on a plant-by-plant basis. In general, blossoms are usually best removed by snipping or breaking them off the stem just underneath the flower. But if this leaves a long unattractive stalk, clip off the stem entirely.

# ONGOING CARE

To keep annuals healthy and prevent the need for extensive renovation, do not overlook the plants' basic requirements. Gardeners sometimes forget that annuals cannot flourish without adequate food, water and light. If any of these are reduced below a generous level, the plants will suffer. This simple reality is difficult for some gardeners to grasp. I would be a wealthy nurseryman if I had a dollar for every customer at our garden center who said, "I don't have to fertilize my plants, I've got good soil."

Our experiments over entire gardening seasons have shown that regular feeding and watering will produce dramatic improvements not only in the number of flowers but also in their size and the vibrancy of their color. Our practice now is to feed annuals a very di-

harder the pinch, the more new shoots will sprout from the plant stem. If cuttings are desired from an overwintered geranium, hard pinching will produce more young, tender shoots for propagation than soft pinching. If a fuchsia in a hanging basket survives the winter and is leggy and pale, a hard pinch will encourage it to fill in quite quickly, while a soft pinch will leave the lower stems bare. Prune artfully—if you cut each stem just above a leaf node, no one but a determined plant detective will ever notice your work.

Pinching also determines the direction in which a plant will grow. For a window box planting, pinch and remove shoots on the house side of the box. This stimulates new shoots that will grow on the outside or "show" side of the box and cascade over the edge in an attractive display.

*Like most annuals, pansies need water and fertile soil in order to renew their display of beautiful blossoms.*

luted liquid fertilizer when we water twice a week. In addition, we apply about ½ inch of compost each fall to improve the soil in the beds. These beds are important to us. Not only are they demonstration and show gardens for our nursery, but they also sustain the plants from which we harvest our seed. We know we can obtain more viable seed from plants that have not been stressed by a lack of food and water, so we make sure they are well irrigated and fed.

We apply liquid fertilizer through our irrigation sys-

tem, but it can be done much more simply. You can obtain wonderful results with a watering can, using manure tea (manure mixed with water) or liquid fish emulsion on a weekly basis. Chapter Ten (page 120) outlines other methods of fertilizing.

Dry fertilizers with a 10-10-10 formulation, meaning 10 percent nitrogen, 10 percent phosphorus, 10 percent potassium and 70 percent inert ingredients, will also provide adequate nourishment for annuals. But we have found that liquid feedings are much more effective during the hot midsummer months when plant growth is relatively slow. The plants can absorb the nutrients more quickly from a liquid source than from a powder. However, lightly sprinkling dry fertilizer around the roots and watering it in is better than not feeding the plants at all. Some gardeners seem to think that fertilizing their annual beds every second or third year is sufficient. But many nutrients are quickly leached from the soil or absorbed by plants. Last year's fertilizer may be of no benefit to this year's plants, so fertilizing annual beds should be a yearly task.

Likewise, watering needs to be a routine part of gardening if annual flowers are to attain their best growth. Like grass, annuals thrive on about 1 inch of water per week. The flowers can make best use of this water if it is provided in two equal installments rather than a single deluge. We timed the sprinklers in our garden to gauge how long it took them to dispense a half inch of water. Now we just turn them on for 40 minutes twice a week and know they are sprinkling the correct amount of water for both the lawns and the gardens. (Different-sized sprinkler heads emit different amounts of water per minute. You can calculate the output of your sprinkler head by setting an old bucket or tub within its range and timing how long it takes to fill the bucket with a half inch of water.)

When you irrigate, don't forget to take natural rainfall into account. Some gardeners rely on automatic timers to activate and shut off their sprinklers. This can lead to scenes of sprinklers twirling away in the middle of a downpour. The extra water won't hurt the garden, but it is wasteful. The fact is, the more attentive you are, the more likely your annuals will flourish. As an old saying in the greenhouse industry puts it, "The person running the hose makes the profit."

If you use a drip irrigation system, you can also calculate how long it will take to deliver a half inch of water to your flower beds. First, determine how much water you need to apply using the following formula: the volume of water needed in gallons = the surface area of the garden x the depth of water needed x 7.5 (the number of gallons in a cubic foot of water). If the garden is 100 square feet and ½ inch of water is needed, the formula would read 100 x 0.5 x 7.5, or 375 gallons. Next, calculate the flow from the drip irrigation system to figure out how long it will take to dispense 375 gallons. Most systems are sold with drip emitters of a given flow rate (such as 2 gallons per hour), but to confirm the output, set the emitter in a 1-gallon container and time how long it takes to fill the container. Multiply that output by the number of emitters in the system. Thirty 2-gallon-per-hour emitters equals 60 gallons per hour, or 1 gallon per minute. A similar approach can be used with a leaky-hose system: Place the hose in a large container, turn on the water and time its output. If it takes five minutes to fill a 5-gallon pail, you know the hose is dispensing 1 gallon per minute. Either system, then, will take 6.25 hours to deliver 375 gallons of water. Once you have figured out the numbers, following through with the irrigation plan is easy. The results of your efforts will be readily apparent—your annuals will respond with lush foliage and cascades of blossoms.

Annuals grown in relatively cool climates are often divided into two classes of hardiness: hardy and half-hardy. Hardy annuals can be sown directly in the garden and require no cold frame or greenhouse protection to start them on their way. Half-hardy seedlings need the protection afforded by a cold frame or greenhouse, or they need an indoor start to allow them to germinate early enough to achieve full flowering before the end of the season.

The following list categorizes more than 80 annuals as hardy (HA) or half-hardy (HHA). The column "Self-Sow" indicates with a "yes" plants that I know to have self-sown in at least one garden in our area (USDA zone 4) for at least two years in a row. They may not self-sow in every garden or every year, but they have done so in at least one site near our nursery. The column "Seeding" indicates whether seeds can be planted outdoors, noted by the word "direct." If indoor planting is recommended, the column lists how many weeks before the last expected frost the seeds should be sown. The last column contains brief comments on the seed or plant.

# RECOMMENDED ANNUALS

| NAME | HA/HHA (HARDY/HALF-HARDY) | SELF-SOW | SEEDING | COMMENTS |
|------|------|------|------|------|
| Adonis | HA | yes | Direct | Germinates easily with direct-seeding. |
| Ageratum | HHA | no | 10-12 wks. | Likes warmth to germinate. |
| Agrostemma | HA | no | Direct | Not widely grown, but a good cut flower. |
| Alonsoa | HHA | no | 8-10 wks. | We save our own seed. |
| Alyssum | HA | yes | Direct or 4 wks. | Never overwintered for me (Zone 4). |
| Amaranthus | HA | yes | 6-8 wks. | Species includes love-lies-bleeding and 'Joseph's Coat'. |
| Anchusa 'Blue Angel' | HA | no | 8-10 wks. | We treat as HHA in our Zone 4 garden. |
| Arctotis | HHA | no | 8 wks. | New species from South Africa. |
| Argemone (most forms) | HA | yes | 6-8 wks. | Thorny; self-sowing; potential weed. |
| Asarina | HHA | no | 6-8 wks. | Good basket plant. |
| Asperula orientalis | HHA | yes | 8-10 wks. | Resembles a weed after a few years. |
| Aster | HA | no | 8-10 wks. | Blooms easily from early sowing. |
| Atriplex hortensis 'Rubra' | HHA | yes | 6-8 wks. | Edible purple leaves. |
| Bachelor's Buttons | HA | no | Direct | Easy to grow by direct-seeding. |
| Basil | HHA | no | 6-8 wks. | Colored-leaved or small-leaved for foliage effect; edible. |
| Bells-of-Ireland | HA | yes | Direct | Does better sown directly early or in cold frame; doesn't like greenhouse heat. |
| Bidens (several forms) | HA | yes | Direct | Excellent flower in ground or container. |
| Brachycome | HHA | no | 6-8 wks. | Small flowers; rots easily. |
| Calendula | HA | yes | 6-8 wks. | Blooms late into fall; a great cut flower. |
| Candytuft (annual species) | HA | yes | Direct | Direct-seeded plants are less leggy than greenhouse starts. |
| Carthamus | HA | no | Direct | Hates greenhouse heat. |
| Castor bean | HHA | no | 6-8 wks. | Provides dense screening; easily grows to 6 feet; poisonous. |
| Celosia | HHA | no | 10-12 wks. | Warm water (to 100 degrees F) accelerates germination and early growth. |
| Chrysanthemum | HA | no | 6-8 wks. | Generally, annual varieties are easy. |
| Clarkia | HA | no | Direct | Very easy and showy. |
| Cleome | HHA | yes | 8-10 wks. | Germinate in cool temperature indoors or in cold frame. |
| Coleus | HHA | no | 10-12 wks. | Grows well with warm water. |
| Collinsia | HHA | no | 4-6 wks. | Not showy but interesting. |
| Coreopsis | HA | yes | 10-12 wks. | A few varieties are perennials but many are annuals. |

| NAME | HA/HHA (HARDY/HALF-HARDY) | SELF-SOW | SEEDING | COMMENTS |
|---|---|---|---|---|
| Cosmos | HA | yes | Direct | Best started in garden. |
| Craspedia | HHA | no | 8-10 wks. | Good for cutting and drying. |
| Crepis | HA | no | 8-10 wks. | Resembles colored dandelion. |
| Cynoglossum | HA | yes | 8-10 wks. | Great blue color. |
| Dahlia | HHA | no | 8-10 wks. | Likes warmth; germinates readily. |
| Datura (all annual species) | HHA | yes | 6-8 wks. | Start in cold frame or greenhouse the first year, then let self-sow. |
| Dianthus (all annual forms) | HA | yes | 10-12 wks. | Cold frames are excellent for germinating. |
| Diascia | HHA | no | 8-10 wks. | Likes warm water. |
| Dimorphotheca | HHA | no | 8-10 wks. | Some have fragrant leaves. |
| Dusty-Miller | HHA | yes | 10-12 wks. | Likes warm water for germinating. |
| Eccremocarpus | HHA | no | 4-6 wks. | Start early for best growth and climbing. |
| Felicia | HHA | no | 8-10 wks. | Interesting blue flower; low-growing. |
| Flowering Cabbage/Kale | HA | no | Direct | Very easy; good fall color; edible. |
| Fuchsia | HHA | no | 10-12 wks. | Start indoors or in cold frame. |
| Gamolepis | HHA | no | 8-10 wks. | Good container plant. |
| Geranium | HHA | no | 12-14 wks. | Start in January for June blooms. |
| Glory Flower | HA | yes | Direct | Easy California poppy. |
| Godetia | HA | no | Direct | Easy if direct-seeded. |
| Gomphrena | HHA | no | 8-10 wks. | Likes warm water to germinate. |
| Grasses (ornamental) | HA | no | Direct | Easy annuals; direct-seed. |
| Gypsophila | HA | no | Direct | Easy annual; baby's-breath. |
| Impatiens | HA | yes | 8-10 wks. | Easy to sow inside or out. |
| Mentzelia | HA | no | 6-8 wks. | Short-lived blooms. |
| Morning-Glory | HHA | yes | 6 wks. | Direct-seed in small pot; do not disturb roots. |
| Nasturtium | HA | no | Direct | Can be started earlier indoors or direct-seeded outside. |
| Nemophila | HA | no | 8-10 wks. | Grow cool. |
| Nicandra | HA | no | 6-8 wks. | Grow cool to avoid stretching. |
| Nicotiana | HHA | yes | 10-12 wks. | Don't cover; pat into soil mix; keep warm. |
| Nierembergia | HHA | no | 8-10 wks. | Once germinated, don't overwater. |
| Nolana | HHA | no | 6-8 wks. | Will bloom sooner if started inside but can be direct-seeded. |
| Omphalodes linifolia | HA | yes | Direct | Self-sows with abandon. |
| Pansy | HHA | yes | 12-14 wks. | Slow germinator and grower. |
| Petunia | HHA | yes | 10-12 wks. | Keep seedlings cool to avoid stretching. |
| Phacelia | HA | no | 6-8 wks. | Easier outside. |
| Phlox | HA | no | 6-8 wks. | Starts better outside in cool temperatures or in cold frame. |

| NAME | HA/HHA (HARDY/HALF-HARDY) | SELF-SOW | SEEDING | COMMENTS |
|---|---|---|---|---|
| Poppy | HA | yes | 6-8 wks. | All annual forms. |
| Portulaca | HHA | yes | 8-10 wks. | Very sensitive to being overwatered. |
| Salpiglossis | HHA | no | 8-10 wks. | Grow cool. |
| Salvia | HHA | no | 10-12 wks. | Deadhead regularly to keep blooming. |
| Schizanthus | HHA | no | 8-10 wks. | Good indoor plant as well as short-blooming outdoor annual. |
| Silene | HA | yes | 6-8 wks. | Can get weedy. |
| Snapdragon | HHA | yes | 10-12 wks. | Very slow to germinate and get started, but a beautiful cutting flower. |
| Statice | HHA | no | 8-10 wks. | Grow cool to avoid stretching. |
| Stock | HHA | no | 8-10 wks. | Cool germinator. |
| Sweet Pea | HA | no | 3-6 wks. | Start in cool temperatures. |
| Sweet William | HA | yes | 8-10 wks. | Prefers cool temperatures. |
| Thunbergia | HHA | no | 6-8 wks. | Vining growth; will climb trellis or cascade from hanging basket. |
| Tithonia | HHA | no | 6-8 wks. | Huge orange blooms. |
| Torenia | HHA | no | 8-10 wks. | Tender; shade-lover. |
| Ursinia | HHA | no | 8-10 wks. | Grow cool. |
| Verbena | HHA | yes | 10-12 wks. | For northern gardeners, too long to germinate and grow in a single season. |
| Violet Cress | HA | no | 6-8 wks. | Small creeper with pale blue blooms. |
| Wahlenbergia | HHA | no | 8 wks. | Blue daisies. |
| Zinnia | HA | no | Direct | Easy to grow by direct-seeding. |

# OVERWINTERING ANNUALS

JUST ABOUT ANY ANNUAL LISTED IN THE CHART above can be maintained over the winter, and cuttings taken from it in the spring can be used to start a new generation of plants. Some of the tall and quick-to-germinate species, such as zinnias or cosmos, might not be worth the trouble as they will not bloom indoors without full sunlight. However, most of the shorter species, including impatiens, geraniums, hibiscus, petunias, torenia, dwarf snapdragons, stocks and pansies, will easily adjust to an indoor setting. Prune the plants to a compact shape for the winter and keep them in a cool, well-lit room. If you cannot provide enough natural light, use fluorescent grow lights—special bulbs with a light spectrum that mimics the sun.

Overwintering annuals may seem foolish or fanatical compared with starting them from seed in the spring, but propagating plants from cuttings, or vegetatively, as the technique is called, ensures genetic similarity with the parent plant. So if you have a favorite geranium or what you think is the perfect shade of snapdragon, you can perpetuate it.

See Chapter Two (page 31) for a description of taking perennial cuttings and constructing a pot-in-pot system to root them. The same process can be followed for annuals.

# COLLECTING SEED

WHILE ANNUALS CAN BE PROPAGATED FROM cuttings, they are most commonly started from seed, which can be collected from a few mature flower heads. Once the flowers are dry, the seeds separate easily from the desiccated petals or seedpods. Clean away chaff, pods, stems and leaves as these can invite decay, and put the seeds in an envelope for winter storage. Label each packet with a nonfading ink—ball-point pens are more reliable than magic markers.

Some people recommend sprinkling milk powder into the envelopes to absorb moisture and keep the seeds dry; other collectors recommend freezing seeds. We have never had any trouble maintaining the viability of our seeds, and we simply put seed-filled envelopes in a cardboard carton and store them in a cool, dry cupboard. A damp area is disastrous for seeds, even if there is milk powder in the container. We make sure the envelopes are completely sealed. Spillage wastes not only seeds but all the work that went into collecting them. If seeds do get spilled, mix them together and broadcast this melange over the spring garden to surprise the neighborhood with a cottage garden floral design.

Knowing when annual seeds are ready to collect is largely a matter of experience, but generally, when the seedpods turn brown, they are ripe for collecting. Seeds from the daisy family are ready when the entire seed head turns brown. Seeds with fluffy, parachute tails, such as tweedia, should be collected when they are just about to be dispersed by the wind. In fact, any seed that separates easily from the plant is likely to be ripe. For us to stay on top of seed collecting, we have to work in the garden from midsummer on with a wad of envelopes stuffed in our pockets. We are always on the lookout for seed that is ready to pick so we can capture it before it parts from the plant on its own.

Plants whose seed overwinters in the garden can be easily established in other locations. (See the chart on pages 16–18 for species that self-sow.) Collect these seeds and spread them around in the fall wherever you want the plants to become established. Do this after you have cleaned up the beds and prepared them for

winter. If the seed fails to germinate the next spring, transplant some of the seedlings that spring up around the mother plant, but don't move the seedlings until they have at least two "true leaves." True leaves resemble the mature leaves of the plant; they do not open until the cotyledons, or first leaves, have unfolded.

# THE SEASON FINALE: GARDEN CLEANUP

HAVING ENJOYED YOUR FLOWERS ALL SUMMER, collected seed and decided which plants will be overwintered indoors, you face the chore of cleaning up the garden. The old maxim about leaving the garden in fall as you want to find it in the spring is as applicable for annual gardens as it is for perennial gardens. However, preparing an annual bed for fall is easier. Pull up the stalks from all the annuals and leave the ground bare. Shred or compost these stalks but do not return them to the garden until they have been completely composted. Otherwise, they might provide habitat for pests and diseases. A rotary lawn mower works well to shred annual flower stalks as long as the stalks are dry. Wet stalks will wrap around the mower blades and stall the machine.

If you spread compost on the beds in the fall, turn it in with a shovel or tiller. This is called rough bed preparation. The objective is to leave the soil with lots of air space rather than trying to create a finely textured seedbed. One pass over the bed with a tiller is enough. Scatter any available leaves over the garden. Most will break down enough so that a quick spring tilling will complete the job, but maple and a few other large flat leaves should be shredded to keep them from matting.

If the annual garden has gotten away from you for the season, fall is an excellent time to begin reclaiming the ground. Simply follow the steps described above and you will leave a clean slate awaiting your return in the spring. After cleaning your gardening tools, you can head indoors with a resolve to begin planning a new annual garden that will be the centerpiece of your landscape.

# CHAPTER TWO

# PERENNIALS

*"And time remembered is grief forgotten,*
*And frosts are slain and flowers begotten,*
*And in green underwood and cover*
*Blossom by blossom the spring begins"*

A.C. SWINBURNE (1837-1909)
***At Parting***

SWINBURNE HAS IT RIGHT. FOR THE PERENNIAL-FLOWER enthusiast, spring is measured "blossom by blossom." The yellow flowers of draba are the first to proclaim the demise of winter, and while their cheerful display is often met with a final dusting of snow, they valiantly reappear above the frosty white blanket and brighten our winter-bound psyches. After draba come the various anemones, then iris, peonies, poppies and other seasonal blooms until the last hardy chrysanthemums of fall.

Perennials are the backbone of the contemporary flower garden. They are, by definition, enduring. Perennial means returning again and again. However, to keep perennial plants healthy and blooming, they must be tended on a regular basis and maintenance rituals must be observed. Much of the perennial gardener's time should be devoted to the three Ds:

*Perennials, such as lupines, irises, daylilies and poppies, are the backbone of the contemporary flower garden.*

digging, dividing and deadheading. Without attending to these down-in-the-dirt chores, you cannot expect your garden to thrive year after year.

Perennial gardening, however, is not entirely labor-intensive. One of the easiest and most rewarding tasks is propagating your own plants. Through a few simple techniques, you can increase your plantings and also pass along a favorite to a friend or acquire a perennial that you admire from another garden. Increasing your stock of perennial plants adds to your gardening responsibilities, but in more than equal measure, it adds beauty to your world.

# DIGGING

IN PERENNIAL GARDENS, RENOVATIONS ARE often made with a shovel. My tool of choice is a round-pointed shovel with a long handle, because it offers a good deal of leverage for dislodging stubborn plants. Digging brings overgrown perennials back to a manageable size, loosens the soil and discourages invading grass. The "big dig" might be another way to describe total bed renovation.

Even in a small bed, a total renovation can be a challenging task, but it is a job that awaits every perennial gardener. Explaining precisely when a bed needs renovation is as difficult as describing how to ride a bicycle. Words are a poor substitute for experience. As a general rule, let me say that a bed needs renovating if the soil is too hard to dig easily with a small trowel, if grass roots have invaded more than one-quarter of your plants or if about one-third of your plants are too large or are dead in the center.

The best time to undertake a complete renovation is in the late summer or fall, depending on where you live. The plants should be at the end of their growth cycle and beginning to shut down for the winter. Yet there should still be enough time for them to become firmly anchored before the arrival of freezing weather.

Otherwise, frost can force them out of the ground. In cold weather climates, including USDA zones 4 and 5, late August through September is the best time to renovate perennials. The plants may still look vigorous and not appear ready to be disturbed but, for the most part, they have finished growing for the year. They will have a better chance of getting established in their new site and will perform better in the spring if the work is undertaken at this time rather than delayed until October.

A complete bed renovation, even in a small garden, can be a time-consuming job. You need to be realistic about how many hours of work you can put in, and then decide whether you can rework all or only part of a bed at any one time. Plants left in a cool, shady area can easily stay out of the ground for several days or even a few weeks if they are dormant. But you do not want to be caught with half your plants still out of the ground when freezing weather arrives.

One of the first steps in bed renovation, certainly if you are a fastidious gardener, is to spread a tarp beside the bed to set your plants on. This will keep plants out of the grass and soil off your walks or lawn.

To dig up plants, set the blade of your shovel 6 to 8 inches away from the outside leaves and work it into the ground. Reaching the right depth is a matter of feel, but essentially, the root will separate from the soil when your shovel is deep enough. Try to lift out the plant with its rootball intact and set it carefully beside the bed.

As you pop your plants out of the soil, don't separate them from their name tags. If a plant doesn't have a tag, write its name on a leaf with a felt-tipped marker. When you begin putting the plants back, you will be rewarded for your time spent trying to keep their identifications straight. Memory can be surprisingly faulty when you have dozens of plants haphazardly arranged next to the garden.

Once the plants are removed, evaluate the mulch on the bed. If it is a deep layer of relatively new material

*The care given to perennials like phlox, poppies and delphiniums is returned in more than equal measure.*

like wood chips, rake it off; if it is old and rotted, you can incorporate it into the bed. Then, proceed to rebuild and double-dig the soil that may be compacted from years of sustaining your plants. (See Chapter Ten, page 120, for a description of soil improvement techniques and double-digging.)

While the renovation project is under way, discourage people and pets from walking on the bed. Set up temporary fencing—even string tied around short stakes—then turn your attention to the plants.

Carefully examine their roots and remove all grass and weeds. Grass is the most invasive plant in many perennial beds. Remove its roots with care. If you overlook even a few grass roots before resetting the perennials, you may face another renovation job in a matter of months. Sometimes the tangle of growth makes it hard to distinguish "good" roots from "bad," so sepa-

rate the roots until you can tell which main root or stalk they belong to. Keep a garbage bag or wheelbarrow handy so you can dispose of the debris. If you overlook weed roots in the cleanup, they will regenerate new plants and new problems in your renovated bed.

When the roots have been cleaned, it is time to choose the fate of each plant. One of the usual goals of renovation is to reduce the number and size of your plants to give each one more room. (The process of dividing plants is covered in the next section.) If your neighbors have been leaning over the fence, providing ongoing commentary and unsolicited advice, politely offer them some of your divisions to give them something to do while you consider your new garden design.

It will never be easier to reorganize. If that *Rudbeckia laciniata* 'Golden Globe' that was planted in the front of the bed is now 8 feet tall, you might want to move it to the back. Shorter plants can be arranged along the front of the bed. Color schemes can be reconsidered. Sketching out your design on paper is an excellent way to see how and where your plants will fit in the renovated space.

Once you have selected all your "keepers," carefully replant them at the same depth that they had been growing. Then, thoroughly water the entire area (enough to create a giant puddle) to anchor the roots and eliminate air pockets in the soil. Irrigate before you spread any mulch on the bed, otherwise the water will not be easily and deeply absorbed by the soil.

In most gardens, applying about 3 inches of mulch is usually sufficient. (See Chapter Eleven, page 130, for a thorough discussion of mulch.) Mulch suppresses weeds, insulates plant roots and retains soil moisture. However, it also prevents many perennials from self-seeding. This is an important means of propagation. If you are among those gardeners who delight in new seedlings, you may want to pull away mulch from certain plants.

After you have mulched the garden, consider systematically labeling the plants. Labeling helps even professionals with identification, particularly with varietal names. Thin white plastic markers are cheap and easy to write on, but they deteriorate quickly. If they are covered with ½ inch of soil, however, they last for many years. Obviously they are not as convenient when buried, but they are easily unearthed for reference. Pressure-treated stakes, particularly the thin, small boards used in lumberyards to separate layers of planks, make suitable and inexpensive labels. A light sanding cleans and smoothes the wood so it can be easily written on with an indelible marker. Plastic tape stamped with raised letters also works well if you staple it to a pressure-treated stake. Without staples, the tape will fall off when the glue on the back deteriorates.

If you want a more attractive, more formal arrangement, you can buy a metal marking system from a garden center or mail-order firm. Using metal labels seems to elevate your plantings to the level of a botanical garden, but it can also create a "graveyard" effect in the fall and winter, when the labels loom above dormant plants like tombstones.

When your work is complete and each perennial is mulched and labeled, you can enjoy the well-ordered garden and delight in the anticipation of spring.

# DIVIDING

THERE COMES A TIME WHEN PLANTS SIMPLY outgrow their allotted space and they must be broken into smaller plants, or divided. Various garden writers have described a cumbersome approach to dividing, which involves digging up the entire plant, carefully prying the roots apart with two garden forks and then replanting a small portion of the roots. This job can be done much more simply with a sharp shovel and a strong arm. Without taking the plant out of the ground, work the shovel vertically into the root mass so you can separate and lift out enough roots to reduce the remaining plant to a reasonable size. Cutting back the roots seldom hurts a plant, and it can provide hundreds of divisions. It is fair to point out that you can probably get more root divisions by carefully separating the roots with two forks than by cutting quickly with a shovel. Nevertheless, with shovel-cutting, the part of the root left in the ground regrows quite nicely and, depending on the plant, will be ready to divide again in another year or two.

If you are skeptical of this technique, try it on any of the plants listed in the chart on the following page. Plants that have been taken out of the ground during a total renovation can easily be divided with a shovel, machete or large knife. There is no need to pry the roots carefully apart; merely cut the plant to the desired size. The plants may be left with bent tops, bruised leaves and chewed-up roots, but have faith—spring brings miracles and renewed growth.

## PLANTS THAT DIVIDE EASILY

| | | | | |
|---|---|---|---|---|
| *Achillea* species | *Bergenia* | *Eryngium* | *Liatris* | *Physostegia* |
| *Aconitum* | *Brunnera* | *Gaillardia* | *Lilium* | *Platycodon* |
| *Ajuga* | *Campanula* | *Geranium* | *Lobelia* | *Polemonium* |
| *Anemone* | *Chrysanthemum* | *Geum* | *Lythrum* | *Primula* |
| *Anthemis* | *Dianthus* | *Gypsophila* | *Mertensia* | *Pulmonaria* |
| *Aquilegia* | *Dicentra* | *Hemerocallis* | *Monarda* | *Rudbeckia* |
| *Artemisia* | *Dictamnus* | *Heuchera* | *Oenothera* | *Tradescantia* |
| *Aster* | *Echinacea* | *Hosta* | *Paeonia* | *Veronica* |
| *Astilbe* | *Epimedium* | *Iris* | *Penstemon* | *Viola* |
| *Baptisia* | *Erigeron* | *Lavandula* | *Phlox* | |

Beginners will find it easier to divide plants in the spring when the new points of growth, or eyes, are apparent as they emerge from the roots or corms. A division needs at least one eye to produce a new plant. Timing is less critical in the spring than in the fall. You do not have to worry about the ground freezing before the plant becomes established. However, any spring divisions should be made while the plants are still small so they will not be badly stressed by the process.

Once gardeners have acquired some expertise in dividing, they can start to follow the general rule governing the seasonal rhythm of the work: If a plant blooms in the spring, divide it in the fall. If it blooms in the fall, divide it in the spring.

## REMEDYING "CENTER DIE-OFF"

Some perennials, such as Shasta daisies or fall-blooming asters, continually produce new shoots from the outside of their root clump. After a few years, they have a large dead spot in the middle of their surrounding greenery and need to be divided. Rejuvenating such plants involves digging them up entirely and cutting out the strong outer clumps from the dead inner core. Make sure that each outer clump carries a healthy and extensive root section. Reset the clumps within a few hours at the same depth the plant was previously growing.

If you cannot replant them right away, keep the salvaged sections in the shade. The roots will last at least a week out of the ground if they are cool, shaded, damp and unfrozen. To promote their survival, cover the roots with a damp towel or wet leaves; plastic is not recommended because heat builds up beneath it.

Invariably, what starts out as a single plant will provide enough new clumps for several gardens. You have to be ruthless with extra divisions. If you replant them all, the perennial garden will soon take on the monotone of a single variety. Instead of trying to accommodate every division, give them to friends, neighbors or the horticultural society plant sale or, in extreme cases, commit them to the compost pile.

## EDGING SPREADING PERENNIALS

Spreading perennials, whether short or tall, work nicely as ground covers, and in mass displays, they can be spectacular. If an individual plant in the center of

## COMMON SPREADING PERENNIALS

| | | |
|---|---|---|
| *Aegopodium podagraria* 'Variegatum' | *Convallaria majalis* | *Lysimachia punctata* |
| *Ajuga* (any variety) | *Geranium thunbergii* | *Oenothera tetragona* |
| *Artemisia pontica* | *Lamiastrum galeobdolon* 'Variegatum' | *Potentilla pleniflora* |
| *Cerastium tomentosum* | *Lamium* | *Sedum acre* |
| *Chrysanthemum serotinum* | *Lysimachia clethroides* | *Vinca minor* |

the mass dies, chop it up with a hoe and neighboring plants will quickly fill in the gap. Once any spreading plants have reached the desired size, use a sharp shovel to trim the edges regularly throughout the season. Also, pull seedlings as soon as you notice them. The culls can be transplanted elsewhere in the garden or given away—be sure to warn other gardeners how aggressive some of these species can be.

Spreading perennials are the bane of my gardening existence. While friends extol their virtues as ground covers and fast and easy garden "fillers," rapidly spreading plants are banished from our gardens. We allowed *Geranium thunbergii* into our main perennial border and this pest (no other word, in my opinion, does it justice) invaded and smothered the *Digitalis ferruginea*, devoured the malvas and battled the iris to a draw—all in three years. It would make a perfect addition to a rough sunny area that needs a ground cover, perhaps behind a barn, but never plant it in a good perennial border.

# DEADHEADING

DEADHEADING MEANS REMOVING SPENT flower blossoms before they set seed. The best technique is to trim off individual flower stalks as low as you can without cutting into the plant's main stalk. Deadheading is an ongoing summer task that should be undertaken for several reasons. It stops seed production, encourages many perennials to continue

blooming and eliminates the old blossoms, which are a potential site for fungal diseases. Deadheading also keeps your perennials attractive and lets the emerging blossoms hold center stage, without competing with a blemished background of dying flowers.

Perennials such as Shasta and butter daisies (*Chrysanthemum* x *superbum* and *Coreopsis lanceolata*) both enjoy an extended bloom period if they are rigorously deadheaded. Deadheading becomes an amusing contest between plant and gardener: the plant wins if it sets seed; the gardener wins by preventing seed formation and thus getting the benefit of more blooms.

Deadheading such plants as delphiniums and cranesbill geraniums immediately after they have flowered will usually encourage them to bloom again later in the season. Fall gardens full of a second set of blue delphinium spires are a joy. Their varied tones of azure are a welcome contrast to the yellows and oranges that dominate most fall gardens. Delphiniums and other repeat-bloomers benefit from a dose of manure tea after their first bloom to strengthen them; without this feeding, their second blooms can be a bit small and straggly.

Deadheading to discourage seed production has two important effects: since seedlings will not germinate the following year, the garden will not become overgrown or need attentive thinning quite so soon and there will be no offspring from modern hybrids. Seedlings from modern hybrids are not genetically identical to their mother plants. If they are allowed to grow, they will change the color and design of the garden. On the other hand, you may want to encourage some seedlings from open-pollinated perennials as insurance in case the parent plant dies. Open-pollinated plants tend to stay genetically consistent, but over the course of several generations, there may be some subtle changes in flower color.

Many gardeners believe deadheading allows a plant to transfer energy from seed production to growth and winter hardiness. However, tests in our gardens (deadheading versus not deadheading) have failed to produce any significant differences in plant health or winter survival. In fact, if a perennial appears to be weakening, it may be a good idea not to pick off the spent flowers and thus allow the plant to set seed. You will then have a source of seedlings to replace the plant if it dies.

Deadheading stands in curious contrast to the idyllic notion of strolling through the perennial garden fill-ing a wicker basket with delicate, colorful flowers for the day's enjoyment; instead, you are filling a wheelbarrow with spent blooms for the compost pile. But deadheading can be a pleasant interlude in an otherwise hectic existence, and it leaves the garden neatly renewed and reminds the plants that a gardener is still in residence.

# NEW PERENNIALS FROM OLD

## SEEDING TIPS

Many short-lived perennials produce large amounts of seed, and it is reasonably easy to germinate a few and transplant the seedlings to replace any plants lost to the ravages of winter. Producing perennials from seed also encourages gardeners to join seed exchanges, whose

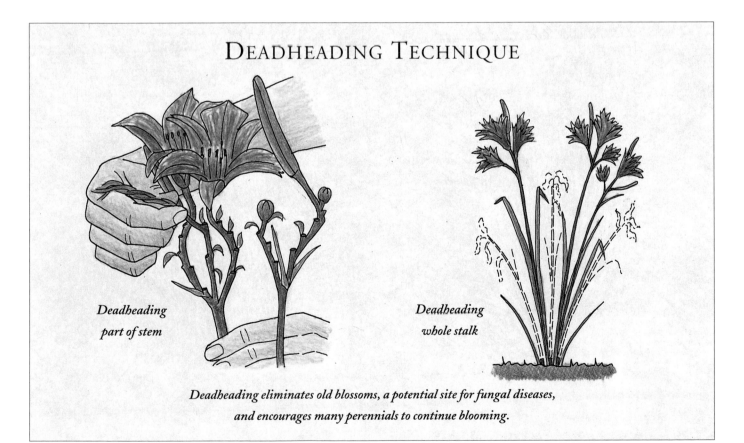

## DEADHEADING TECHNIQUE

*Deadheading part of stem*

*Deadheading whole stalk*

*Deadheading eliminates old blossoms, a potential site for fungal diseases, and encourages many perennials to continue blooming.*

members are dedicated growers who swap seeds of their prized or obscure plants.

The gardener should understand that perennial seeds are a bit different from annual flower seeds. With annual seeds, the fastest germinator gets a head start on life, and with this head start comes an increased chance of survival. In contrast, perennial plants have other survival strategies: they set a lot of seed but only a few will naturally germinate in any given year. It would seem that the parent plant wants to ensure genetic survival but prevent too much competition for food and water.

Delayed germination is caused by a hard seed coat that must be broken by the elements and by the seed's hormonal clock. This impervious coat can take between two weeks and decades of alternating winter and summer conditions before it cracks and allows the seed to germinate.

The process can be hastened and the germination rate often increased substantially by nicking, or scarifying, the seed coat. Even a little nick with a jackknife or file will accelerate germination. If the seeds are numerous or too small to hold, try this technique: Wrap a sheet of 100-grit sandpaper around the inside of a jar with the abrasive side facing in. Then, pour in the seeds and spin and shake the container until the seed coats are lightly scratched. This will allow water to reach the interior of the seeds more quickly and the germination process to begin.

The easiest way to germinate perennial seeds is to simply plant them in the garden in fall and let Mother Nature do the work. Ninety-nine percent of all viable perennial seeds will germinate with this approach. The cold winter temperatures followed by warmer spring conditions set off hormonal changes in the seed that promote germination. Make sure to mark the planting site so that you do not inadvertently weed out the seedlings in the spring.

Another simple germination method involves filling 4-inch flowerpots with a sandy planting mix that will not compact over the winter. (Compacted soil has no air spaces to allow for small developing roots.) Pour boiling water onto the soil until the water comes out the drainage holes. This sterilization kills weed seed and disease organisms. Then plant the seeds at least ¼ inch apart; closer spacing may encourage disease. Only the largest seeds, such as lupine or hollyhock, need to be covered with soil. Sprinkle a very thin layer of chick grit over smaller perennial seeds to maintain even humidity around the newly germinating seed embryos. (Chick grit is finely milled stone often sold at farm supply stores and fed to chickens to help them grind up their food.) This constant humidity is critical in the early germination phase if the plant is to survive, and chick grit is ideal for retaining the needed moisture. If chick grit is not available where you live, try a light layer of sterilized sand, fine gravel or ground brick, sometimes called turface. This thin covering also holds the seed in place if you accidentally flood the pot while watering. (Initial waterings with a mister are recommended.) Label each pot using a plastic tag and an indelible marker. Old plastic margarine tubs can be cut to make tags.

Place the pots outside in a shady spot—with each pot buried to its rim in the soil—to pass the winter. Shade keeps the soil mix from drying out as quickly as it would in the sun. Shaded pots will also remain snow-covered for longer in the spring. The more snow the better for insulation, so the budding seedsman should not be afraid to pile snow over the assembled pots. In the spring, the only attention these pots will need is to be kept uniformly damp (not waterlogged). Common perennials germinate very easily and bountifully under this system.

Once a seedling has at least four true leaves (leaves that look like those on the mature plant), it is a good idea to transplant it to its own pot before moving it

*The varied flower tones and foliage textures of irises captivate the eye and lift the spirit.*

into the rough and tumble of the garden. A perennial is large enough to transplant when its roots have reached the edge of the pot. Check to see if the plant has reached that size about two weeks after you have transferred it to its own pot: While supporting the plant, turn the pot upside down and gently ease the soil ball out. If the roots are white to the edge, plant the perennial in the garden; if there are no roots in evidence, give the plant another two weeks. If the roots have not reached the edge of the pot in a month, there is not enough food in the soil. Begin feeding the seedling each week with a half-strength solution of liquid plant food.

Some of the more unusual perennials often take two years to germinate. If you have the space and the patience, keep the seed mix moist all summer and leave it outside for a second winter. Some determined and optimistic gardeners will leave seeds outdoors for several years, but in most cases, if a common perennial does not germinate after its first winter, it will probably never sprout. Some special plants are worth your patience, and if these plants are in your garden, you will appreciate the value of waiting.

One other technique worth mentioning for the home gardener is the use of hot water. When seeding perennials in the spring, the *initial* watering can be very hot. Using the water straight from the tap at its hottest will speed up the germination of many spring-sown perennials, especially *Aquilegia* species.

Watering the seed trays with lukewarm water is another good technique for improving seed germination. Using warm water (the temperature of a baby's bath is perfect) helps prevent the sudden drop in soil temperature caused by cold tap water. Imagine yourself as a germinating seed—you would surely appreciate the pleasant feeling of warm water rather than cold.

For a more controlled and often higher rate of germination than with outdoor fall planting, start perennial seeds in containers in the early spring. Sow the seeds in flats of sterilized soil, water the flats and put them outside for two to three weeks of wet, freezing weather, which will help break the seeds' dormancy. Then, bring the containers inside to a warm, well-lit area and maintain the soil temperature at 72 degrees F. Soil temperature is invariably 10 degrees cooler than the surrounding air temperature, so try to find places in your house where the air temperature is above average; likely spots are near radiators or woodstoves, on top of some refrigerators (feel the top for warmth before committing a flat to that location) or on an electric warming pad. Keep the soil damp but not waterlogged. Overwatering will often cause seeds to rot. This is especially true of seeds that do not have a hard coat or that have a tail. Most indoor seed germination will occur within 90 days. If a seed has not germinated during that time, repeat the process, using your refrigera-

## PLANTS THAT GROW EASILY FROM ROOT CUTTINGS

| | | |
|---|---|---|
| *Aconitum* | *Echinops* species | *Limonium* |
| *Anchusa azurea* | *Eryngium* species | *Papaver orientale* |
| *Anemone japonica* | *Filipendula* | *Phlox paniculata* |
| *Anemone pulsatilla* | *Gaillardia* species | *Primula denticulata* |
| *Asclepias tuberosa* | *Geranium* (many of the | *Salvia* species |
| *Brunnera macrophylla* | species) | |

tor as a "weather box" for two to three weeks to simulate damp, cold conditions.

One final caveat on starting perennials from seed: Just barely cover the seeds with planting medium. Burying seeds too deeply is the primary cause of germination failure. In my experience, planting seeds ¼ inch deep (as many seed packages recommend) or at a depth of three times their width (as many gardeners favor) is too deep. My suggestion is to bury a seed to a depth equal to its width, if you bury it at all. We cover our seeds with just a dusting of chick grit—a layer so thin that the tops of larger seeds poke through—and our germination rates are very satisfactory. Bear in mind, however, that the shallower the planting depth, the more quickly a seed can dry out and the more important it is to keep the planting medium moist.

## ROOT CUTTINGS

Many perennials can be successfully propagated from root cuttings. Some gardeners have discovered this inadvertently by moving a clump of tall perennial phlox (*Phlox paniculata*) and finding that the plant resprouted from part of the roots left in the old location. In fact, with Oriental poppy (*Papaver orientale*), root cuttings are the best method of obtaining another plant that is true to the original. As any poppy grower knows, poppies seed themselves with abandon. But because the seed includes genes from two parents, the offspring will not be genetically true to any one plant. Should you want to give a poppy to your neighbors, root cuttings are the best and easiest way to make sure the color and form of the plant remain constant.

Timing is critical to the success of root cuttings. You have to take the cutting when the plant is dormant. For beginners and home gardeners, very early spring is the best time to undertake this chore. The easiest way is to dig a clump of the parent plant out of the center of the large root mass and cut away roots that are about as thick as a pencil and 2 to 4 inches in length. (Cut-

tings that are too thick may be old and inactive; if they are too thin, they do not have adequate food reserves to sprout and root.) Meanwhile, fill three-quarters of a 4-inch-diameter flowerpot with sterilized potting soil. Lay a root section horizontally in the flowerpot and cover it with ½ inch of loose topsoil. Water with lukewarm water. Keep the soil warm and slightly damp. Water sparingly, or rot will ruin the cutting. New shoots will appear in one month; transplant them into the garden after all danger of frost has passed.

## TOP CUTTINGS

Taking a cutting from one of your favorite plants and giving it to a friend is a time-honored tradition in horticulture. The perennial garden, in particular, is a sharing garden, one from which the delights of the senses can be passed along to those with a similar passion for plants, those with the affliction known as "perennialitis."

A cutting is a section of tip growth that is usually 3 to 5 inches long. Taking a cutting at the right time is the first step to ensuring that it will root successfully. Ideally, the tip growth should be soft and pliable but not watery. You should be able to bend it about 90 degrees and have it snap cleanly from the stem. If the tip growth bends 140 or 150 degrees before snapping, it is too soft and not ready for rooting. If it bends and then crimps instead of snapping, it is too woody and has hardened beyond the optimum stage. Cuttings have a chance of rooting even if they are younger or older, so if a friend offers, take the cutting regardless of the season and try to get it to root.

Keeping a cutting moist is another critical step toward success. The more wilted a cutting becomes, the less likely it is to root. To ensure that your cuttings are as turgid (full of water) as possible, take them early in the morning. Cuttings made later in the day, when the level of moisture in the plant is lower, are less likely to succeed. Regardless of when a cutting is taken,

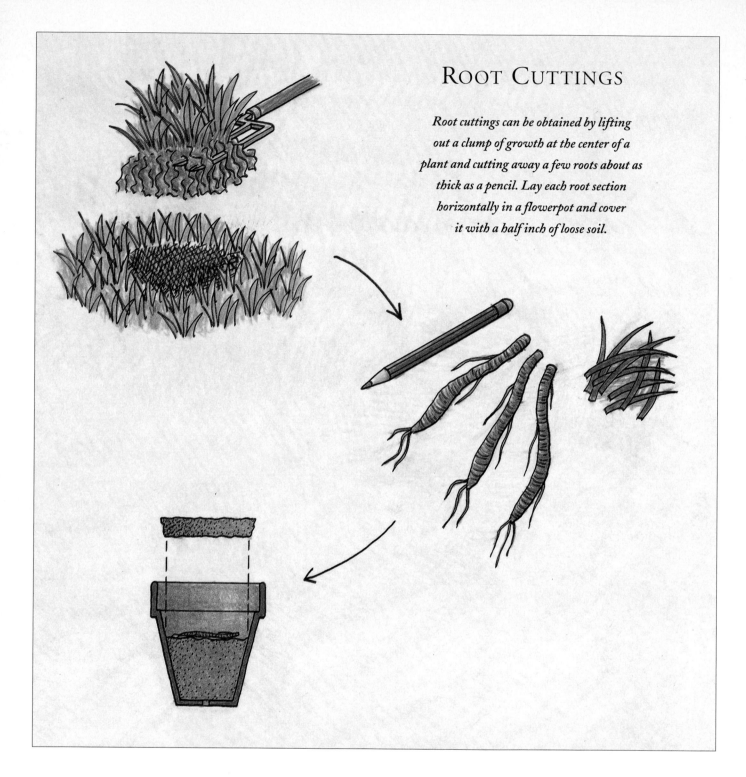

## ROOT CUTTINGS

*Root cuttings can be obtained by lifting out a clump of growth at the center of a plant and cutting away a few roots about as thick as a pencil. Lay each root section horizontally in a flowerpot and cover it with a half inch of loose soil.*

spraying it with an antidesiccant, either before or after it has been harvested, is an excellent way to prevent wilting. An antidesiccant is a liquid wax that seals the pores on leaves, preventing them from losing moisture. If water is conserved in the leaves, most cuttings will root much more easily. There are several antides-iccants on the market sold under different trade names. Your garden center probably stocks at least one. Gray-leaved plants are particularly sensitive to moisture loss, and applying an antidesiccant may be the only way to get such cuttings to root. An antidesiccant can also be the salvation of donated cuttings that might have been taken at the wrong time of day or be suffering from a long, hot car trip.

Sealable plastic bags can also enhance the survival of any plant material—simply pop a fresh cutting into a bag and seal it. (Make sure you write the name of the plant on the bag with a magic marker.) I carry a whole roll of plastic bags in my camera case so that if cuttings or divisions are offered to me on a garden visit, I can keep the gift viable until I get home. When we are away from home for several weeks, I keep cuttings in the refrigerator of our camper, where they stay fresh and vital.

Before you put a cutting in a container of potting soil, trim it to a length of 3 to 5 inches if necessary. Short cuttings (less than 1 inch) also root, but they require more consistent care than is often given at home. Before planting, remove the leaves from the bottom half of the cutting. This will prevent them from rotting and infecting the stem. Bury one-half of the length of the cutting in your soil mix.

Soil mixes for propagating cuttings need a great deal of air space so that young roots can easily become established. One very good propagation mix consists of three parts of a commercial soilless mix to one part perlite. You can also use three parts sterilized potting soil mixed with one part sand or perlite.

Once the cutting is placed or "stuck" in the soil, the major challenge is to prevent moisture loss. To accomplish this, you must keep the rooting medium uniformly damp but not soggy.

Soil moisture can easily be maintained with a propagation system put together from two clay plant pots. The smaller pot serves as a water reservoir; the larger holds the soil. The smaller pot should fit comfortably in the larger one—there should be at least 2 inches between the rims of the pots. Seal the drainage hole in the smaller pot with a glue gun. Partially fill the larger pot with soil, and set in the smaller pot so the top of its rim is approximately level with the rim of the larger pot. Then, fill around the smaller pot with more soil. Keep

## TWO-POT PROPAGATION SYSTEM

*In a two-pot system, the smaller pot is filled with water and nestled into the soil of the larger pot. Moisture seeping through the walls of the smaller pot keeps the soil evenly damp, encouraging the plant cuttings to root.*

the smaller pot filled with water; water seeping through the pores of the smaller pot will ensure that the soil stays uniformly moist. Set the cuttings in the ring of soil between the edges of the two pots.

To prevent the cuttings from wilting, keep them out of the sun and spray them with an antidesiccant if you haven't already. (One application of antidesiccant will last until the cutting has rooted.) Putting a white plastic bag loosely over the cuttings will also serve to reduce moisture loss from the leaves.

Cuttings root at different times—between 5 and 45 days from the time they are set in the medium is average for perennials. A very gentle tug on the top of the cutting will determine rooting progress—if there is resistance to the tug, then rooting has begun. Be gentle when testing—too much tugging can destroy

## PLANTS THAT GROW EASILY FROM TOP CUTTINGS

| | | |
|---|---|---|
| *Achillea* | *Gypsophila* | *Phlox* species |
| *Artemisia* (taken when the plant is only 5 inches tall) | Herbs (some varieties, such as mints and sages) | *Physostegia* |
| *Aster* | *Iberis* | *Salvia* species |
| *Chrysanthemum* species | *Lamium maculatum* | *Sedum* |
| *Coreopsis verticillata* | *Lysimachia* species | *Thymus* |
| *Dianthus* species | *Monarda* species | *Veronica* |
| *Geranium* species | *Penstemon* | |

newly formed roots. New growth from the top of the cutting is a sure sign that rooting is well under way. Evaluate each cutting separately, as there is great variation in rooting speed—some cuttings will be out in the garden for a month before their companions root. If leaves start to fall off a cutting, it is unlikely it will ever root. However, keep the cutting in the rooting medium until the last leaf has dropped—as long as it has foliage, there is hope it will root.

# PEONIES— SPECIAL PERENNIALS

Peonies can be among the most striking, long-lived and reliable of garden perennials. However, the appearance of their huge spherical blossoms—in tones ranging from cream, to pink to dusky maroon—should not be taken for granted. Peonies have a few unusual qualities or horticultural requirements that distinguish them from other herbaceous perennials and merit special attention.

Planting depth is critical. While most perennials are relatively forgiving and do not demand to be planted at a precise depth, peonies should be set quite close to the surface. They should be planted with the eyes, or growth points, on their roots no more than 1 inch deep. (Eyes are the hard, pointed, usually reddish-colored future sprouts that are visible along the roots.) If a peony is planted any deeper, it will produce lush foliage but no blooms. An established peony that is not flowering may be encouraged to bloom simply by raising the roots so that the eyes are closer to the surface.

Peonies can also be more challenging to divide and transplant than many other perennials. They resent being moved and will often sulk for a year or two afterward without blossoming. However, their bloom cycles are less apt to be disturbed if the plants are moved in the fall rather than in the spring. Putting them into warm fall soil helps their roots establish more quickly than they do in cooler spring temperatures.

Peony roots are massive and well anchored compared with other perennials. More than one impatient gardener has snapped a shovel handle trying to pry a plant out of the ground. Despite their tenacious hold in the soil, peony roots are surprisingly brittle. It is difficult to move a mature plant without its roots breaking into a dozen pieces. This will not be harmful to the plant, but if you leave the peony in the shade for an hour or two after you dig it up, the roots will soften a bit and be less likely to break with subsequent handling.

Peonies can be left in the ground and easily divided by cutting away a root section. As long as each root chunk contains an eye, it should eventually become a flowering plant. However, the more eyes on the division, the faster it will return to flowering.

Peonies can be grouped into two broad categories: garden varieties derived from *Paeonia lactiflora* and tree peonies of the *Paeonia suffruticosa* family. Both thrive in similar growing conditions: they prefer full sun or very light shade and soil with a near-neutral pH. While they do tolerate alkaline soils with a pH above 7.0, they do not flourish in acidic soil, which is commonly found near conifer and oak trees.

Both forms of peonies benefit from feeding. A ¾-inch layer of compost or aged manure applied in the spring will enhance blossoming. A balanced fertilizer with a 10-10-10 formulation may also be ap-

plied. When the buds begin to form, water the plants with manure tea. Garden varieties thrive in northern areas (USDA zones 4 and 5) with an additional light mulch applied in the fall to retain soil moisture and protect the crowns from freezing and thawing before the arrival of an insulating blanket of snow.

Being so long-lived, peonies sometimes become shaded by trees that were small when the peony was planted. The gradual decrease in sunlight often means fewer and fewer blossoms. Moving the plant to a sunnier spot may be all that is needed before it will again produce an abundance of beautiful, fragrant flowers. Properly planted and cared for, a peony will last the life of the gardener; it seldom needs renovating unless the garden conditions around it change.

*Though delicate-looking, peonies are long-lived and reliable perennials when their horticultural requirements are met.*

# PERENNIAL PLANT RENOVATION

T HE FOLLOWING TABLE OF PERENNIALS, organized by Latin names, is included for general reference. The performance of each plant will differ in individual gardens. What will need renovating in a garden with poor soils in four to five years may require renovation after only two or three years in a more fertile site.

The plants listed here are those commonly found in garden centers. There may be several varieties for each listing, but in most cases, all of the varieties will have similar growth habits.

*Achillea filipendulina*
**(yarrow)**
**When to renovate:** Every four to five years, if center dies out.
**How to renovate:** Simple division, discarding old dead pieces; easily propagated from tip cuttings or self-seeding. This species is variable in color so that tip cuttings or root divisions are best.

*Achillea millefolium*
**(yarrow)**
**When to renovate:** Every four to five years, or when center dies out.
**How to renovate:** This variety is extremely variable in color, so once a good clone is found, it should be propagated from tip cuttings. Easily divided in early spring or early fall.

*Aconitum napellus*
**(monkshood)**
**When to renovate:** Every four to five years or when too large.
**How to renovate:** Easily divided in early fall. Pieces of root left in ground will sprout the next year, so if plant is to be moved, take all roots or dig up again in spring.

*Agastache foeniculum*
**(anise hyssop)**
**When to renovate:** Every two to three years.

**How to renovate:** Self-sows prolifically; weed out extra seedlings.

*Ajuga reptans*
**(bugleweed)**
**When to renovate:** Seldom requires total renovation. Individual dead plants in clump may have to be removed in spring, but clump will quickly fill in on its own. Edge at any time to control growth.
**How to renovate:** Use a sharp shovel to contain spreading roots and remove wayward offshoots. Root pruning can be done at any time of year.

*Alcea nigra*
**(black hollyhock)**
**When to renovate:** Seldom.
**How to renovate:** Make sure chipmunks do not eat seed; self-sows.

*Alchemilla mollis*
**(lady's-mantle)**
**When to renovate:** When clump gets too large for desired bed.
**How to renovate:** This plant loves to self-sow; dig up new plants to control size of clump.

*Allium cernuum*
**(nodding pink onion)**
**When to renovate:** When clump gets too large.

**How to renovate:** Use a sharp shovel to control size of clump and to remove self-sown plants.

*Anaphalis margaritiacea*
**(pearly everlasting)**
**When to renovate:** If too large.
**How to renovate:** Dig up extra plants; self-sows.

*Anchusa azurea*
**(alkanet)**
**When to renovate:** Seldom; when old plants die out.
**How to renovate:** Big taproot, difficult to move. Self-sows or can be propagated from root cuttings in fall and overwintered in cold frame or pot sunk in soil. Do not dig up too early in spring if it appears dead.

*Anemone pulsatilla*
**(anemone)**
**When to renovate:** Every three to five years.
**How to renovate:** Allow to self-sow or propagate root cuttings.

*Anthemis tinctoria*
**(golden marguerite)**
**When to renovate:** Every two to three years, center dies out.
**How to renovate:** Divides easily; self-sows. Cull seedlings to control spread.

*Aquilegia* x *hybrida*
**(columbine)**
**When to renovate:** Seldom; if mother plant dies out.
**How to renovate:** Self-sows. Always keep babies coming; will spread around garden on its own if seedpods are left to dry.

*Arabis alpina*
**(rock cress)**
**When to renovate:** Every three to five years, center may die out.
**How to renovate:** Clean out dead foliage in spring.

*Armeria maritima*
**(thrift)**
**When to renovate:** Seldom; if mother plant dies out.
**How to renovate:** Self-sows.

*Artemisia ludoviciana*
**(silver-king)**
**When to renovate:** Every three to five years, remove dead areas.
**How to renovate:** Sharp shovel will limit this plant's growth. Renovate when too large by edging. Interior dead spots will be filled by new growth.

*Artemisia pontica*
**(Roman wormwood)**
**When to renovate:** Seldom.
**How to renovate:** Will perpetuate itself if new growth is allowed to spread.

*Artemisia schmidtiana*
**(silver mound)**
**When to renovate:** Every three to five years, depending on winter damage.
**How to renovate:** Make root divisions in spring with a sharp shovel; take pieces with tight silver foliage just showing at base of old dead stalks.

*Aruncus dioicus*
**(goatsbeard)**
**When to renovate:** Every ten years or more.
**How to renovate:** Divide with a shovel in spring or fall when clump is too large. Takes several years to reestablish its height and spread.

*Asclepias tuberosa*
**(butterfly weed)**
**When to renovate:** Seldom; if mother plant dies.
**How to renovate:** Resents transplanting; allow to self-sow.

*Asphodelus luteus*
**(King Solomon's spear)**
**When to renovate:** Every five years or more.
**How to renovate:** Self-sows; dig up shoots or new seedlings to limit spread.

*Aster alpinus*
**(alpine aster)**
**When to renovate:** Every two to three years.
**How to renovate:** Parts of clumps continually die out. Self-sows. Dig out dead parts after blooming in spring and replant the healthy rooted clumps.

*Aster tongolensis*
**(alpine aster)**
**When to renovate:** Every three to five years when center dies out.
**How to renovate:** Self-sows. Discard dead center section in spring; replant healthy rooted clumps.

*Astilbe arendsii*
**(spirea)**
**When to renovate:** Every ten years or more.
**How to renovate:** Medium- to slow-growers. Simply cut off chunk containing two to three eyes in early spring or fall and replant.

*Aubrieta deltoidea*
**(false rock cress)**
**When to renovate:** Every two to three years.
**How to renovate:** Short-lived in our garden; collect seed to replant. Some divisions can be moved in very early spring to replace dead spots.

*Aurinia saxatilis*
**(golden-tuft alyssum)**
**When to renovate:** Every two to three years.
**How to renovate:** Very short-lived in our garden; allow to self-sow or collect seed to replant.

*Baptisia australis*
**(false indigo)**
**When to renovate:** Every five years or more.
**How to renovate:** Start from seed. Young plants look similar to peas. Divisions are difficult because of taproot but can be made if done carefully in spring.

*Bergenia cordifolia*
**(bergenia)**
**When to renovate:** Every five years or more.
**How to renovate:** Start new plants from seed, offshoots or divisions; seed is easiest. Plant in late spring.

*Campanula carpatica*
**(tussock bellflower)**
**When to renovate:** Every three to five years.
**How to renovate:** Plant vigorously self-sows; not a question of renovating but of limiting growth. New plants quickly cover any that have died. Remove dead growth in spring.

*Campanula grandiflora*
**(Canterbury-bells)**
**When to renovate:** Every two

*Planting perennials like yarrows and delphiniums in combination enhances visual interest.*

years; plant is biennial.
**How to renovate:** Self-sows if happy in spot.

### Centaurea dealbata
**(bachelor's-button)**
**When to renovate:** Every five years or more.
**How to renovate:** Center rarely dies, but if it does, renovate in spring. Easily divided if gets too large. Self-sows with abandon.

### Centaurea macrocephala
**(bachelor's-button)**
**When to renovate:** Every three to five years.
**How to renovate:** Self-sows; rarely needs division in our garden but can be divided if too large.

### Centaurea montana
**(mountain bluet)**
**When to renovate:** Yearly.
**How to renovate:** Self-sows with abandon; seedlings require constant weeding or will take over garden.

### Cerastium tomentosum
**(snow-in-summer)**
**When to renovate:** Every two to three years.
**How to renovate:** Edge with shovel constantly or it will become invasive. Do not allow into formal garden.

### Chelone glabra
**(turtlehead)**
**When to renovate:** Every five years or more.

**How to renovate:** Slow-spreader; makes a nice clump. Can divide when too large.

### Chrysanthemum coccineum
**(pyrethum)**
**When to renovate:** Every three years when center dies out.
**How to renovate:** Dig out center, dig up extra babies, replant.

### Chrysanthemum x morifolium
**(mum)**
**When to renovate:** Every two years when center dies out.
**How to renovate:** Modern hybrids do not winter well. With old-fashioned varieties, the center part of the plant may die and need to be removed each spring.

## *Chrysanthemum parthenium*
**(feverfew)**
**When to renovate:** Every two to three years when center dies out.
**How to renovate:** Dig up dead center plant and replace with smaller plant at edge of clump.

## *Chrysanthemum serotinum*
**(giant daisy)**
**When to renovate:** Every two to four years.
**How to renovate:** Edge to control the spread. Dig up any dead center plants; the rest will colonize.

## *Chrysanthemum* x *superbum*
**(Shasta daisy)**
**When to renovate:** Every two to three years when center dies out.
**How to renovate:** Dig up dead center plant. Replace with smaller plants at edge of clump.

## *Cimicifuga racemosa*
**(black snakeroot)**
**When to renovate:** Every five years or more.
**How to renovate:** Any dead areas can be dug up; the remainder of the large root will expand into this area.

## *Convallaria*
**(lily-of-the-valley)**
**When to renovate:** Every three to five years, if any part winter-kills.
**How to renovate:** Winter damage can be dug or hoed up. Rest of colony will fill in with no assistance.

## *Coreopsis lanceolata*
**(coreopsis)**
**When to renovate:** Every two to three years. Short-lived.
**How to renovate:** Self-sows; encourage seedlings.

## *Coreopsis verticillata*
**(coreopsis)**
**When to renovate:** Every five years or more.
**How to renovate:** Long-lived plant. Needs very little work.

## *Delphinium elatum*
**(delphinium)**
**When to renovate:** Every three to five years.
**How to renovate:** Encourage seedlings. Dig out dead or massive old clumps to encourage two- to three-year-old heavy-flowering clumps.

## *Dianthus* x *alwoodii*
**(clove pink)**
**When to renovate:** Every two to three years. Short-lived.
**How to renovate:** Encourage seedlings. Survival of mother plant depends on winter snow cover.

## *Dianthus barbatus*
**(sweet William)**
**When to renovate:** Every two years; plant is biennial.
**How to renovate:** Encourage seedlings. Can become weedy.

## *Dianthus caryophyllus*
**(carnation)**
**When to renovate:** Every two to five years.
**How to renovate:** Encourage seedlings. Do not cut back but cover with snow or mulch in winter.

## *Dicentra eximia*
**(bleeding-heart)**
**When to renovate:** Every three to five years.
**How to renovate:** Dig up dead center plants; replace in spring with new plants at edge of clump. Feed well to establish.

## *Dicentra spectabilis*
**(bleeding-heart)**
**When to renovate:** Every five years or more.
**How to renovate:** Edge with a shovel to control. Self-sows.

## *Digitalis purpurea*
**(foxglove)**
**When to renovate:** Every two years; plant is biennial.
**How to renovate:** Thin out self-sown seedlings.

## *Echinacea purpurea*
**(purple coneflower)**
**When to renovate:** Every two to three years.
**How to renovate:** Weed out poor-flowering specimens that have self-sown.

## *Eryngium amethystinum*
**(sea holly)**
**When to renovate:** Every three to five years.
**How to renovate:** Dig out seedlings regularly; self-sows vigorously.

## *Euphorbia epithymoides*
**(spurge)**
**When to renovate:** Every five years or more.
**How to renovate:** Thin out self-sown seedlings.

## *Gaillardia* x *grandiflora*
**(blanket flower)**
**When to renovate:** Every two to three years. Short-lived.
**How to renovate:** Encourage self-sown seedlings.

## *Geranium macrorrhizum*
**(cranesbill)**
**When to renovate:** Every five years or more.
**How to renovate:** Edge with shovel when control is necessary. Rarely dies out in center.

*Geum*
**(avens)**
**When to renovate:** Every two to three years.
**How to renovate:** Short-lived in cold climates. Encourage seedlings.

*Gypsophila paniculata*
**(baby's-breath)**
**When to renovate:** Every five years or more.
**How to renovate:** Rarely needs renovation. Relax and enjoy it.

*Gypsophila repens*
**(baby's-breath)**
**When to renovate:** Every two to three years. Short-lived.
**How to renovate:** Self-sows; encourage seedlings to fill in winter-killed spots.

*Hemerocallis*
**(daylily)**
**When to renovate:** Every ten years or more.
**How to renovate:** Use a shovel to limit growth. A no-work plant other than deadheading.

*Hesperis matronalis*
**(dame's rocket)**
**When to renovate:** Every three to five years.
**How to renovate:** Dig up seedlings to limit spread in garden.

*Heuchera sanguinea*
**(coralbells)**
**When to renovate:** Every three to five years.
**How to renovate:** Center may die. Take cuttings of good varieties to replace dying plants.

*Hosta*
**(hosta)**
**When to renovate:** Every ten years or more.

**How to renovate:** Divide to control spread or renew blooming.

*Iberis sempervirens*
**(edging candytuft)**
**When to renovate:** Every three to five years.
**How to renovate:** Shear yearly to encourage thick growth. Cuttings root easily or will self-sow.

*Iris* x *germanica*
**(iris)**
**When to renovate:** Every two to three years.
**How to renovate:** Dig and divide when clump gets too crowded.

*Lathyrus latifolius*
**(perennial pea)**
**When to renovate:** Every five years or more.
**How to renovate:** Allow to self-sow.

*Lavandula angustifolia*
**(lavender)**
**When to renovate:** Every five years or more.
**How to renovate:** Prune in spring to remove winter-kill. Cuttings root easily or will self-sow.

*Lavatera cachemiriana*
**(tree mallow)**
**When to renovate:** Every three to five years.
**How to renovate:** Self-sows; encourage seedlings.

*Linum lewisii*
**(flax)**
**When to renovate:** Every year.
**How to renovate:** Control by weeding. Self-sows prolifically. Clump slowly expands and spreads.

*Lobelia cardinalis*
**(cardinal flower)**
**When to renovate:** Every three to

five years.
**How to renovate:** Encourage seedlings. Dig out and replace with younger outside plant if center dies.

*Lobelia siphilitica*
**(blue cardinal flower)**
**When to renovate:** Every three to five years.
**How to renovate:** Weed to control; self-sows heavily.

*Lunaria annua*
**(silver-dollar)**
**When to renovate:** Every two years; plant is biennial.
**How to renovate:** Weed to control; self-sows heavily.

*Lupinus* x *hybridus*
**(lupine)**
**When to renovate:** Every three to five years.
**How to renovate:** Weed to control. Self-sows and will transplant easily once established.

*Lychnis chalcedonica*
**(Maltese-cross)**
**When to renovate:** Every two to three years.
**How to renovate:** Self-sows; encourage seedlings. Once established, weed to control.

*Lysimachia clethroides*
**(gooseneck loosestrife)**
**When to renovate:** Every five years or more.
**How to renovate:** Edge to control once size is adequate. A vigorous spreader.

*Lysimachia nummularia*
**(creeping Jennie)**
**When to renovate:** Every five years or more.
**How to renovate:** Edge to control once size is adequate.

*If perennial renovation is done regularly, plants like poppies, lupines and irises will respond with a profusion of flowers.*

### Malva
**(mallow)**
**When to renovate:** Every two to three years.
**How to renovate:** Self-sows prolifically. Weed to control.

### Monarda didyma
**(bee balm)**
**When to renovate:** Every five years or more.
**How to renovate:** Edge to control. Very fast spreader.

### Myosotis sylvatica
**(forget-me-not)**
**When to renovate:** Every two years; plant is biennial.
**How to renovate:** Self-sows heavily. Dig up clumps for friends.

### Nepeta x faassenii
**(catmint)**
**When to renovate:** Every three to five years.
**How to renovate:** Propagates easily from cuttings. Some self-sowing.

### Oenothera fruticosa
**(sundrop)**
**When to renovate:** Every three to five years.
**How to renovate:** Self-sows; encourage seedlings.

### Oenothera pallida
**(evening primrose)**
**When to renovate:** Every two years; plant is biennial.
**How to renovate:** Encourage self-seeding.

### Papaver orientale
**(Oriental poppy)**
**When to renovate:** Every five years or more.
**How to renovate:** Self-sows unless deadheaded. Control by weeding. Root cuttings establish easily.

### Penstemon barbatus
**(beard-tongue)**
**When to renovate:** Every two years; plant is biennial.
**How to renovate:** Self-sows. Control size of bed by weeding. Can propagate by cuttings.

### Petrorhagia saxifraga
**(tunic flower)**
**When to renovate:** Every two to three years.

*Delphiniums, daylilies, phlox and other perennials return year after year to brighten the landscape.*

**How to renovate:** Control it if you can by weeding. Hoe up dead areas; encourage to fill in by self-sowing.

### Phlox paniculata
**(perennial phlox)**
**When to renovate:** Every five years or more.
**How to renovate:** Control by edging with shovel.

### Phlox subulata
**(moss pink)**
**When to renovate:** Every five years or more.
**How to renovate:** Occasionally winter-kills, hoe out dead patches and allow to recolonize. Cuttings root easily.

### Physalis alkekengi
**(Chinese-lantern)**
**When to renovate:** Every three to five years.
**How to renovate:** Control by weeding regularly; very invasive.

### Physostegia virginiana
**(false dragonhead)**
**When to renovate:** Every five years or more.
**How to renovate:** Dig and remove center if dies out; replace with new plants at edge of clump.

### Phyteuma nigrum
**(horned rampion)**
**When to renovate:** Every three to five years.

**How to renovate:** Self-sows. Replace dead mother plant with baby.

### Platycodon grandiflorus
**(balloon flower)**
**When to renovate:** Every five years or more.
**How to renovate:** Rarely needs attention; self-sows. Replace dead plants with seedlings.

### Potentilla pleniflora
**(creeping cinquefoil)**
**When to renovate:** Every five years or more.
**How to renovate:** Center may die. Hoe dead spot and mass will recolonize. A vigorous spreader.

*Primula cortusoides*

**(Siberian primrose)**

**When to renovate:** Every three to five years.

**How to renovate:** Self-sows. Allow seeds to dry on pod and spread in desired area.

*Primula japonica*

**(Japanese primrose)**

**When to renovate:** Every three to five years.

**How to renovate:** Allow to self-sow. Requires damp site.

*Pulmonaria montana*

**(lungwort)**

**When to renovate:** Every five years or more.

**How to renovate:** Divide to replace any dead zones.

*Rudbeckia newmanii*

**(black-eyed Susan)**

**When to renovate:** Every two to three years.

**How to renovate:** Encourage to self-sow, then weed to control.

*Salvia argentea*

**(silver sage)**

**When to renovate:** Every two to three years.

**How to renovate:** Encourage self-sowing. Dig out and replace dead mother plant.

*Saponaria ocymoides*

**(soapwort)**

**When to renovate:** Every three to five years.

**How to renovate:** Encourage self-sowing. Cuttings root easily.

*Saxifraga caespitosa*

**(London pride)**

**When to renovate:** Every three to five years.

**How to renovate:** Self-sows. Hoe out dead parts, transplant or sow seeds to for replacement growth.

*Sedum kamtschaticum*

**(sedum)**

**When to renovate:** Every five years or more.

**How to renovate:** Rarely dies but if patch is dead, hoe out and it will recolonize. Can be easily propagated from cuttings.

*Sedum spectabile*

**(ice-plant)**

**When to renovate:** Every five years or more.

**How to renovate:** Dig and divide.

*Sempervivum*

**(hen-and-chicks)**

**When to renovate:** Every five years or more.

**How to renovate:** Easy to dig and divide.

*Stachys byzantina*

**(lamb's-ears)**

**When to renovate:** Every three to five years.

**How to renovate:** Dig up babies and use to replace winter-killed areas. Self-sows and spreads.

*Thermopsis caroliniana*

**(Carolina lupine)**

**When to renovate:** Every three to five years.

**How to renovate:** Allow to self-sow.

*Thymus serpyllum*

**(wild thyme)**

**When to renovate:** Every three to five years.

**How to renovate:** Allow to self-sow.

*Tradescantia virginiana*

**(common spiderwort)**

**When to renovate:** Every three to five years.

**How to renovate:** Encourage seedlings in damp areas or plant root cuttings.

*Verbascum chaixii*

**(mullein)**

**When to renovate:** Every two to three years.

**How to renovate:** Allow to self-sow but be selective. Seedlings can be variable in color. Dig up poor ones.

*Veronica longifolia*

**(long-leaf Veronica)**

**When to renovate:** Every three to five years.

**How to renovate:** Allow to self-sow or propagate from cuttings. Remove dead clumps.

*Veronica teucrium*

**(germander speedwell)**

**When to renovate:** Every three to five years.

**How to renovate:** Propagate from cuttings because it self-sows sparsely.

*Vinca minor*

**(common periwinkle)**

**When to renovate:** Every five years or more.

**How to renovate:** Use root divisions to replace any dead plants. Weed to control spreading.

*Viola cornuta*

**(horned violet)**

**When to renovate:** Every two years.

**How to renovate:** Allow to self-sow or propagate from cuttings or root divisions. Control by weeding or edging.

*Viola cucullata*

**(marsh blue violet)**

**When to renovate:** Every five years or more.

**How to renovate:** Control growth by edging. Rarely dies but the odd winter damage can be hoed and recolonized. Dig to multiply.

CHAPTER THREE

# *F*LOWERING

# SHRUBS

*"If you can't be a pine on the top of the hill,*
*Be a scrub in the valley—but be*
*The best little scrub by the side of the rill*
*Be a bush if you can't be a tree"*

G. WITHER (1588-1667)

*A Love Sonnet*

I

IN OUR RECOLLECTIONS OF HOME, OF RELATIVES OR OF A
time of life, flowering shrubs are often a dominant theme. Lilacs
summon thoughts of my grandmother, who filled her house each
spring with their perfumed flowers. Forsythia reminds me of
my mother. Her triumph was a large, spreading bush, cascad-
ing with yellow blossoms, which she raised from a cutting not much
longer than her finger.

More so than herbaceous perennials, flowering shrubs have a year-
round presence in the landscape. Entire garden designs can be based on
a few striking plants—the sheer volume of blossoms on a large honeysuckle or spirea can be stunning. The foliage, too, has ornamental qualities, from the first pale green leaves of spring to the yellow and orange or
crimson tones of fall. And in winter, the structure of the shrubs' branches

*Entire garden designs can be based on a few striking flowering shrubs, such as lilacs.*

continues to lend visual interest to any setting.

Flowering shrubs are often enjoyed from a distance and left to fend for themselves, or at the opposite extreme, they are overpruned and turned into caricatures of plants. From either a lack or an excess of pruning, a potentially charming shrub can dominate or destroy an otherwise attractive landscape.

Flowering shrubs benefit from care, and part of that care involves proper pruning. As with trees (Chapter Seven, page 84), there are two kinds of pruning cuts for shrubs—each encourages a different response from the plant. A thinning cut removes an entire branch back to where it started as a bud. No further growth will occur from that site. A heading cut removes only part of a branch, back to a bud somewhere along its length. This will increase the amount of wood produced by the shrub because it promotes sprouting from buds along the remaining section of the branch. Nonselective heading cuts, or shearing, will thicken the growth on the outside of a bush. Thinning cuts, on the other hand, open up the center of a shrub and make it look more natural.

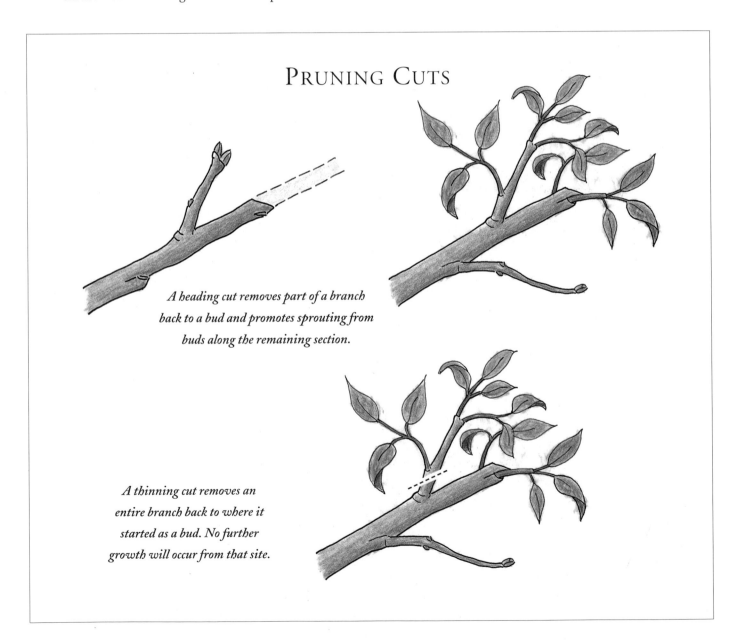

# PRUNING CUTS

*A heading cut removes part of a branch back to a bud and promotes sprouting from buds along the remaining section.*

*A thinning cut removes an entire branch back to where it started as a bud. No further growth will occur from that site.*

# PRUNING STRATEGY

A NODE IS THE BOTANICAL NAME FOR A PLACE where a leaf or side branch joins a stem. When pruning, nodes are used as points of reference. Try to keep each cut ⅛ to ¼ inch above a node, toward the tip of the branch. The closer to the node you cut, the less stub you will leave. Long stubs will wither and give the shrub a sickly appearance.

In the plant world, nodes fall into three categories: alternate (where there is a node on one side of a stem, then a space and another node on the other side); opposite (where the nodes emerge in pairs along the stem); and whorled (where three or more nodes emerge in a circle around the same part of the stem). Simple observation will show that the majority of plants in the garden have alternate nodes or leaf patterns. These are the simplest to prune neatly because you can position the shears quite close to each node.

Stems with opposite nodes can be more challenging. The V formed by the leaves or stems sometimes interferes with getting your pruners close to the node. One technique for making a cleaner cut in such circumstances is to prune off the inward-growing leaf or stem of the pair, as well as the main stem. This will also open up the center of the plant.

Plants with a whorled node pattern are not common in the garden, but they can be neatly pruned—they are easy to cut just above a node.

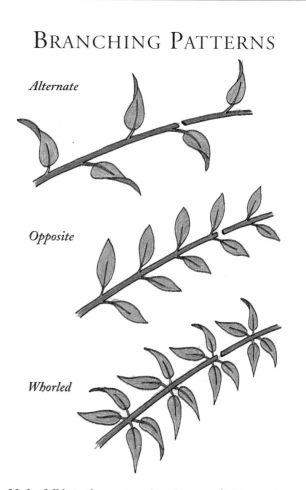

## BRANCHING PATTERNS

*Alternate*

*Opposite*

*Whorled*

*Nodes fall into three categories: alternate (with a node on one side of a stem, then a space, then another node on the other side); opposite (with the nodes emerging in pairs along the stem); and whorled (with three or more nodes emerging in a circle around the same part of the stem).*

# RENOVATING AN OLD SHRUB

R ENOVATION PRUNING, AS OPPOSED TO annual maintenance, is easier on the gardener and the shrub if it is undertaken in the dormant season, after the leaves have fallen. The framework of the shrub will be clear, and the plant will not respond to pruning by setting tender growth that could easily be winter-killed. The first and most satisfying step in restoring an old shrub is to get rid of the dead wood. It can be a long job (especially on a big, old shrub), but once finished, the plant will take on a new life. Getting rid of the dead wood using thinning cuts also means eliminating the withered, unsightly stubs left by previous pruners.

Dead branches are not difficult to distinguish from live ones. Typically, their bark does not have the sheen of living bark, and the buds on dead branches are flattened or shriveled. Also, dead wood is a different color.

# PRUNING OLD SHRUBS

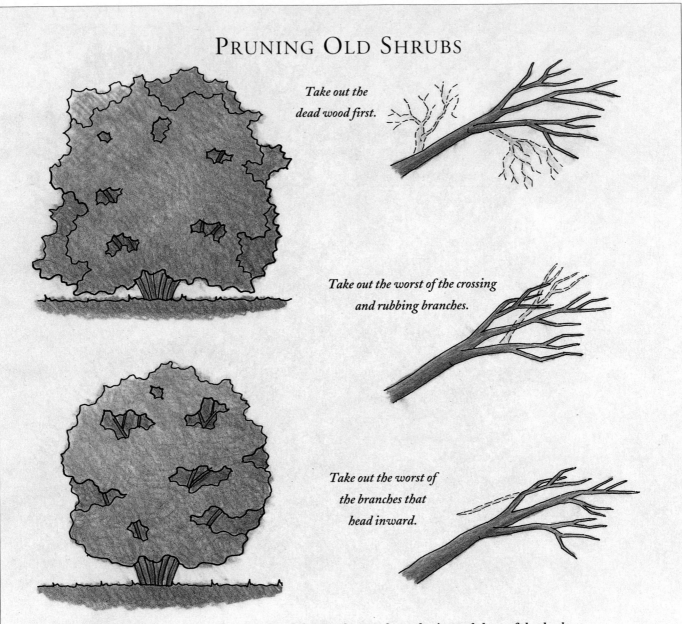

*Take out the
dead wood first.*

*Take out the worst of the crossing
and rubbing branches.*

*Take out the worst of
the branches that
head inward.*

*In the course of pruning, stand back frequently to evaluate the size and shape of the shrub.*

(The color varies from shrub to shrub.) If dead wood is scratched with a sharp tool, it will show brown or black layers beneath the bark. Live wood will be green.

After the dead wood has been cut away and cleared from around the base of the shrub, take a careful look at the remaining branches. Ask yourself if the shrub is the right size and shape for its location. If you decide more pruning is warranted, step back and examine your work after every few cuts. There is no "right" or "wrong" size for a shrub; it depends on the garden, the plant and, most importantly, the gardener.

If the plant has to be reduced further, the second step in renovating is to use thinning cuts to remove all crossing and rubbing branches. Begin with the largest pairs of branches and work toward the smaller ones. In each case, spare the healthier or best-placed branch. After each cut, stand back and evaluate the size and shape of the shrub. If you have cut away too much, don't worry, the shrub will grow back.

If the shrub still requires renovation, eliminate any branches that grow toward the interior of the shrub. This inward growth, from the largest down to the smallest twigs, will not get enough light to develop fully and is the next generation of crossing and rubbing branches. Start with the largest and work progressively toward the smallest. Remember to step back regularly to evaluate your work. Having removed all the dead, crossing, chafing and inward-growing branches, the shrub will look better and be more structurally sound. Further reducing its size takes the job from the science to the art of pruning. Which branches are to remain and which are to be removed will depend on the gardener's aesthetic sense. There are no meaningful guidelines that can be given in a book; simply practice, examine the effect and practice some more.

## MAINTENANCE PRUNING

ANY NORMAL MAINTENANCE PRUNING ON A flowering shrub must be timed to the plant's bloom cycle. The general rule is: Shrubs that bloom in the spring on old wood should be pruned immediately after they flower. These include daphne, flowering almond, forsythia, lilac, purple-leaved sand cherry and silverbell. If the shrub blooms in the summer on new wood, prune in the dormant season or early spring. These shrubs include buffalo berry, elder, potentilla, spirea, viburnum and weigela. It is important to remember that this is maintenance pruning. More involved renovation pruning should be done during the dormant season. It may reduce the blossoming in the first year on some early-spring flowering types, but it should stimulate new growth and more flowers in subsequent years.

Gardeners sometimes ask if they can avoid all the branch-by-branch pruning and instead simply cut a shrub back to the ground and let it start again. The answer depends on the type and growth habit of the shrub. If the shrub grows from a single stem, like some dogwoods or hybrid lilacs, cutting it to the ground will likely either kill it or encourage it to send out multiple stems. None of these stems will produce a good shrub without extensive pruning, so it will take longer and be just as much work to try to renew certain shrubs by cutting them to the ground. However, if the shrub grows by sending out multiple shoots from ground level, such as hydrangea, forsythia, common lilac, mock orange, spirea, weigela or elder, cutting it back to a height of 12 to 18 inches may be a good strategy. It will take several years for the plant to reach a respectable size (given enough food, water, winter protection and weeding), but this works as a lazy gardener's approach to renovating an overgrown shrub.

On the other hand, some big old shrubs, such as monstrous honeysuckles, will sometimes not throw new shoots when cut to the ground; instead, they may die. If an old giant has no leaves on the first 3 to 4 feet of its trunk, then chain-saw renovation may produce firewood, not a rejuvenated plant.

My suggestion is, instead of hacking any plant off at half its height, be patient and prune in a branch-by-branch fashion. The work is enjoyable and the results will be quite satisfying.

## PRUNING FOR A NATURAL LOOK

SOMETIMES PEOPLE BUY A HOUSE AND INHERIT flowering shrubs that have all been sheared to a very even, perhaps boring, shape, and they may want to let the plants achieve a more natural form. Encouraging this transformation is straightforward. If you look at the shrub, you will see that the branches in the outer layer are very small and twiggy. The cuts that produced this shape are shearing or heading cuts, so use thinning cuts to promote a natural look.

First, eliminate any dead wood and crossing branches. Once you have improved the plant's structure, you can begin to prune for natural shape using this approach: Look at all the places on the shrub where branches fork. If the fork has three or more fingers, cut out the middle one(s). Leave only the two outside forks.

Start at the outside of the shrub, with the twiggy growth at the end of each branch (growth that loosely resembles a dinner fork). Use thinning cuts to remove all middle tines, or twigs, from each fork.

Then begin working toward the middle of the shrub, into the next-larger layer of branches. Find the side branches, or sublaterals, that support the outer forks you just finished pruning. Follow the sublaterals back to the forks from which they originated. If these

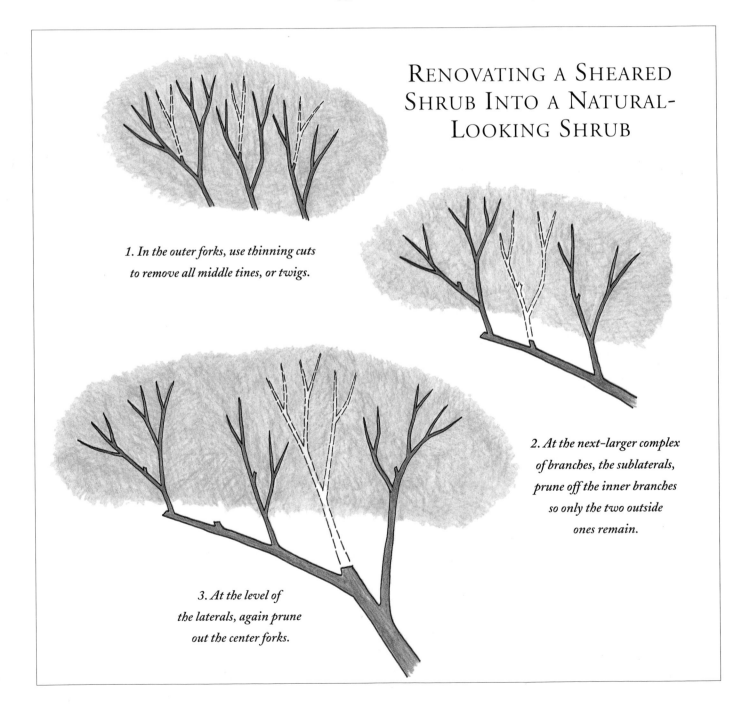

## RENOVATING A SHEARED SHRUB INTO A NATURAL-LOOKING SHRUB

*1. In the outer forks, use thinning cuts to remove all middle tines, or twigs.*

*2. At the next-larger complex of branches, the sublaterals, prune off the inner branches so only the two outside ones remain.*

*3. At the level of the laterals, again prune out the center forks.*

forks have three or more tines, prune off the inner ones so only the two outside branches, or tines, remain.

Now move farther into the shrub, to the next-larger complex of branches—the laterals. Again, prune out the center forks of this growth.

Once you have thinned three levels of branches, the shrub should appear more natural in shape. With the worst of the twiggy growth removed, the shrub will be free to grow in its own way. Regular pruning should then be done as needed to keep the shrub free of dead, crossing and chafing branches.

# MOVING OR PROPAGATING OLD SHRUBS

OLD SHRUBS CAN BE EASILY MOVED, BUT before you get out the shovel, consider several factors. The first is timing. Ideally, shrubs should be moved when they are dormant. Early spring or late fall is best.

If you have to transplant a shrub at the height of the growing season to spare it from, for instance, construction equipment, water it thoroughly for several days before the move and, before you begin to dig, coat both sides of the leaves with an antidesiccant. This is a type of wax that will seal the leaves enough to minimize their moisture loss. The plant will resent the disturbance, but with extra care and the antidesiccant, it should endure.

After moving the plant to its new location, the key to survival is providing adequate water. Copious amounts are needed in all but heavy clay soils. Five gallons a day for the first two weeks and then 5 gallons every second day for four weeks is a good start. After this start-up schedule, water with 5 gallons twice a week. This amount can be cut in half for heavy clay soils. Another way of watering is to let the garden hose trickle at the base of the shrub for several hours twice a

week for the first two months and once a week after this for the remainder of the summer.

Successfully moving any shrub is largely dependent on how much of the roots you are able to move intact. Get help if necessary to ensure you are taking as many roots as possible. One approach for moving larger shrubs is to dig a trench around the drip line of the plant, two shovels wide and two shovel blades deep. Undercut the trench at the base to form a rootball and shift the shrub onto a piece of plywood, heavy cardboard or an old sheet or tarp. Use this support to drag the shrub to its new home.

Sometimes a flowering shrub is in declining health or is too large to move. In such cases, its contribution to the landscape need not be lost forever. It can be used to propagate new, genetically identical plants. Take cuttings from the old shrub in late spring or early summer, when the new growth is quite young and "soft." Generally, a cutting between 3 and 5 inches long is ideal. If you take your cuttings when the new growth on the branch tips is about that length, they should have the right amount of softness to root quickly. The cuttings can be rooted using the two-pot system described in Chapter Two (page 33). In my experience, the two-pot system works almost as well as my commercial misting system to keep cuttings damp and to promote rooting. In the case of gray-leaved plants, such as members of the artemisia family, the two-pot system actually works better. Once the cuttings are well rooted (test by pulling on them gently), you can transplant them to their new home.

Propagating your own flowering shrubs is one of the most satisfying accomplishments in horticulture. Cuttings may have come from a favorite shrub at your former home and provide a feeling of familiarity at your new residence, or they may be from the home of a friend or relative. By encouraging a tiny cutting to take root and blossom, you are preserving not only plant material but also the wonderful associations that accompany a particular plant from a special place.

CHAPTER FOUR

# ROSES

*"Any nose,*
*May ravage with impunity a rose"*

ROBERT BROWNING (1812–1889)
*Sordello VI*

WHEN IT COMES TO CULTIVATING ROSES—
the most prized of garden flowers—debates
rage about the best techniques for planting,
pruning and renovating them. Ardent growers around the world often insist on the supe-
riority of their particular approaches and may even dismiss anyone who
fails to follow their examples. But in my view, rose culture is no place
for dogmatism. There is no single "best way" to raise a rose. Every garden is different, and while general growing guidelines are useful, every
gardener must learn what will work for her or him. I successfully grow
roses in my gardens in Ontario. My approach should be applicable in
other cold-winter gardens, but even in milder areas, some of my growing techniques may be useful.

Many reference books go into great detail on the parentage of roses
and the different levels of care each species requires. But what difference does parentage make when what is most important is how each rose
is tended? If a plant looks and behaves like a cluster or shrub rose, treat

*Roses reward experimentation. Every gardener must learn which techniques will succeed in a particular site.*

# ROSE ANATOMY

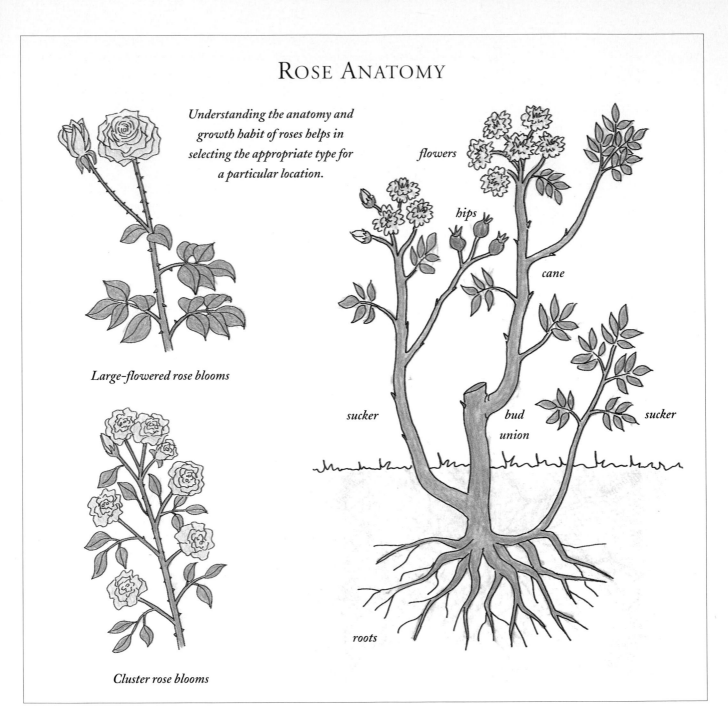

*Understanding the anatomy and growth habit of roses helps in selecting the appropriate type for a particular location.*

flowers

hips

cane

sucker

bud union

sucker

roots

*Large-flowered rose blooms*

*Cluster rose blooms*

it like a cluster or shrub rose. If it has the growth and blooming habit of a large-flowered rose, prune and renovate it accordingly. Large-flowered roses are mainly modern hybrids—teas, hybrid teas and their various crosses. They bear large single blossoms. Cluster or shrub roses (the terms are used here interchangeably) bear their flowers in clusters. They tend to be less highly bred than the large-flowered roses (as they are often species roses rather than hybrids), and

they grow in a bush or shrub form. While there may be exceptions to this rule, a beginning gardener cannot go wrong pruning a large cluster rose as if it were a large bush.

Despite the demure beauty of their flowers, roses can be unruly plants. Gardeners with limited space may, at some point, say of one of their roses, "It's too big, too woody, too old or too much trouble to divide—it's time to start over." Should this occur, there are simple propagation techniques described below, as well as tips for pruning and dividing, that will allow any gardener to make sure the plant continues to thrive in the garden without becoming an overwhelming element.

## GOOD GROWTH

BEFORE JUMPING INTO THE TOPIC OF renovating roses, it is important to understand the basics of good rose care. No matter how well a gardener prunes a rose, if its fertility and cultural needs are not met, the rose will bloom less profusely. This short summary will serve to remind us of what roses demand if they are to achieve their full potential.

Roses will grow in a wide range of soil conditions, however, a medium-heavy loam with a pH of 6.5 is ideal. Roses will also grow in light, sandy soil as long as they are regularly watered. What roses will not en-

dure is poor drainage, often found in heavy clay soils. If their roots are waterlogged, they will not grow. Adding sand or organic matter to clay soil will lighten the structure and make the ground more suitable for roses' probing roots.

Roses require fertile soil for bountiful flower production. When planting, it is important to work copious amounts of compost or composted manure (fresh manure burns tender plant roots) into the soil. Applications of phosphorus-rich fertilizers, such as bone meal, are wonderful for root development.

All large-flowered roses need a spring feeding of bone and blood meal or other complete rose fertilizer and then weekly or biweekly feedings of weak manure tea when they begin to bloom. (Whether the applications are weekly or biweekly depends on your time and energy.) The large cluster or shrub roses are less demanding than delicate tea types and simply require their spring feeding of compost, plus bone and blood meal.

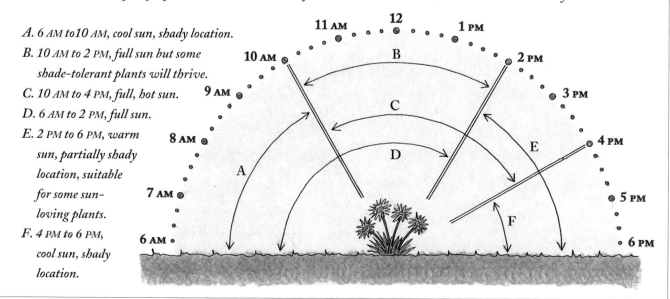

## WHAT IS SUN, WHAT IS SHADE?

*The quality of sunlight a plant receives varies not only with the total length of exposure but with the time of day the light is received. An hour of morning sun is less intense than an hour at midday. The accompanying key describes six different exposures, or times, when a plant might receive sunlight and defines the value of each in terms of sun and shade. For example, if a plant receives direct sun only between 6 AM and 10 AM, it is said to be in a shady location.*

*A. 6 AM to 10 AM, cool sun, shady location.*
*B. 10 AM to 2 PM, full sun but some shade-tolerant plants will thrive.*
*C. 10 AM to 4 PM, full, hot sun.*
*D. 6 AM to 2 PM, full sun.*
*E. 2 PM to 6 PM, warm sun, partially shady location, suitable for some sun-loving plants.*
*F. 4 PM to 6 PM, cool sun, shady location.*

While roses thrive in many different kinds of soil, they will not bloom well unless drenched in sunshine; they require at least six hours of "hot" sun a day, and the more the better. Rarely will roses thrive if tucked up against a north wall. The simple rule is: "Plant roses in full sunlight."

One of the problems facing the roses in our front-house garden is the encroaching shade as our chestnut and crabapple trees mature. We can expect a slow decline of these rose bushes, and we will need to renovate the beds, move the roses and make an entirely new shade garden within the next few years. Encroaching shade from maturing trees is something that many gardeners overlook in their evaluation of why plants are no longer growing "as they used to," so keep this in mind when you are planning a renovation.

# CLUSTER OR SHRUB ROSES

OLD SHRUB ROSES ARE AN ACQUIRED TASTE in the world of rose gardening. Their bloom time is shorter than that of the modern hybrids, their fragrance is more subtle and they can grow into 15-foot giants covered with forbidding thorns. Suckering, self-seeding, prone to many rose diseases and full of virus infestations, these roses are the bane of modern rose fanciers. But to those of us who appreciate them, old shrub roses are the cream of the crop. Who can fail to be amazed by a 'Harrison's Yellow' in full bloom with its fragrant clouds of yellow flowers? Or what about a *Rosa glauca*? It sends forth cascades of two-toned pink blossoms, which give way to hundreds of brilliant red hips or seedpods that enchant us all fall and winter. Once a bush rose becomes established, the aspiring rosarian will delight in its hardiness and generous display.

Critics of cluster roses point out that the bloom time is fleetingly short. These critics do not mention the brief blooming of, say, forsythia or lilac. Length of bloom time is hardly relevant when the beauty, fragrance and hardiness of the plant are being consid-

ered. Besides, many of the cluster roses bloom sporadically all summer, and it is partly these modest but repeated displays that keep it fully blooming in our mind's eye long after the season has passed.

## PRUNING

It can be argued that the most successful pruning strategy for cluster or shrub roses is no pruning at all. Merely allowing these woody shrubs to take their natural course is the easiest and best gardening technique. In the main borders at our nursery, an old *Rosa glauca* has never been pruned, yet it continues to flower profusely year after year.

The beginning gardener should understand that wildly contorted growth is natural for many of the cluster roses and that a relaxed attitude toward rose pruning and renovation is recommended. In an informal garden, shrub or cluster roses rarely need attention

## PRUNING CLUSTER ROSES

*Pruning out the oldest canes every winter to leave between three and seven stalks will help maintain a vigorously flowering plant.*

# HOW SHRUB ROSES GROW

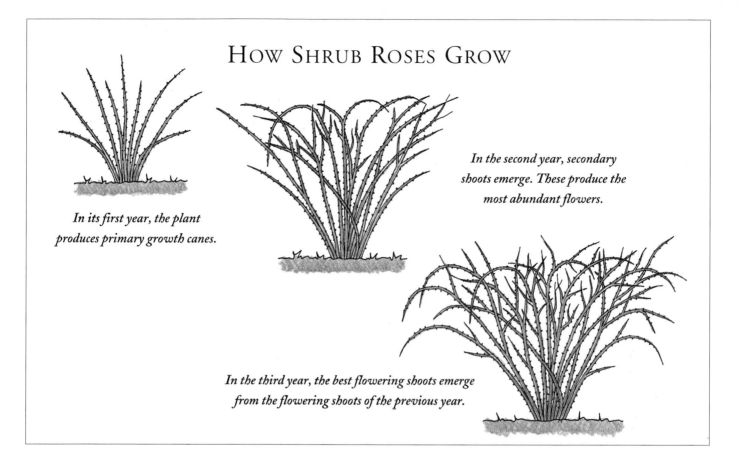

*In its first year, the plant produces primary growth canes.*

*In the second year, secondary shoots emerge. These produce the most abundant flowers.*

*In the third year, the best flowering shoots emerge from the flowering shoots of the previous year.*

other than pruning out dead wood when the plant is dormant (without leaves). In more formal or smaller gardens, the practice of shortening last year's flowering canes by one-third to one-half their length during the winter months will help keep the plant within bounds and promote new, thicker growth. The size can also be controlled by pruning out some of the main stalks. The fewer canes coming from ground level, the smaller the shrub will be. Pruning out the oldest canes every winter to leave between three and seven stalks will help maintain a vigorously flowering and good-sized shrub.

## GROWTH

In its first year, the shrub rose throws up primary growth canes. In the second year, secondary shoots grow from these original canes, and it is these secondary shoots that give us the best flowering. In the third year, the best flowering shoots come from last year's flowering shoots. This process continues until the canes are too thin, too crowded or just worn out.

They subsequently deteriorate and die. Annually pruning out the four- to five-year-old wood at the base of the plant will alleviate the need for the renovation procedures outlined below.

## RENOVATION

Due to age or a lack of attention, cluster roses, even in naturalized settings, sometimes need remedial work. In more formal gardens, they require gentle but frequent attention with pruning tools. The following steps will help maintain a pleasing shape.

### Step One

When the rose is dormant, cut out all dead wood. Invariably, some of these dead canes will be found in the center of the plant. To determine if a cane is dead or alive, lightly scratch the bark with a knife or shears. If the layer right under the bark is brown, the stalk is dead; if the layer is green, the stalk is alive. You will quickly learn how deep to scratch to find live tissue.

Beginners are sometimes hesitant to scratch live stems, but it helps if you look at the procedure this way: dead stems are not hurt by scratching deeply and live stems will be spared from being needlessly pruned off. Small scratches on bark will quickly heal (see Chapter Seven, page 86, for modern approaches to wound dressing).

There are numerous theories on how many main stalks to leave on the shrub. If they are pruned at all, shrub roses in our garden are pruned to leave three to five main stalks. But keep in mind the main rule for pruning: If in doubt, don't cut it out. The corollary to this rule is that a shrub rose is very forgiving and if you make a mistake, it will not be serious.

### Step Two

Remove all weak shoots that will not support clusters of blossoms. There are few things as depressing in the garden as the sight of weak stems sagging under the weight of blossoms.

### Step Three

Eliminate crossing or rubbing branches by pruning one of the branches back to its point of origin. Opening up the center of the rose bush allows for more air circulation, and hence a healthier plant. When eliminating chafing branches, cut out only one of the touching canes. Generally, the older of the two is the one to eliminate.

### Step Four

Thin out overcrowded areas to keep the stems from becoming leggy. Thinning enables the remaining canes to become stronger and better able to support the weight of a cluster of blossoms.

### Step Five

Shorten long, arching canes. When they are old, these long canes do not throw new buds or flowers quite as prolifically as younger canes. Pruning them can encourage the growth of more productive wood. A neophyte pruner has two options in the case of large, old wood: either remove it all immediately, or remove half the first year and see what happens. If the rose

*Climbing roses pose a particular challenge to gardeners in cold climates, but success can be both eye-catching and fragrant.*

does not throw many new buds from the cane lengths that remain, completely prune the older canes the following dormant season.

As you embark on your renovation, remember to do severe pruning in the dormant season. (Falling leaves signal the beginning of dormancy, while swelling buds and the reappearance of leaves indicate the end of the dormant period.) Light pruning of spent flower stalks can be done during the summer. Following these simple guidelines will create a more open plant, with fewer dead or old canes in the interior. The plant will be more attractive and productive.

If a grower is tending a large old rose in a small garden, there are two quick and simple renovation steps to keep the plant in scale with its surroundings. First, follow the instructions above, thinning canes and eliminating all dead and crossing branches. Second, reduce all canes in height by one-third to reduce the shrub to an appropriate size. Cutting back the canes will force more lateral growth from the main canes; prune this new lateral growth back quite hard the following winter. (Pruning quite hard means reducing the length of each new lateral flowering cane significantly, leaving only 3 to 5 inches of new cane.) These short laterals will produce slightly fewer flowers, but the flowers will be of better quality. By following these suggestions, the shrub rose will be reduced in size quite quickly and the subsequent growth will be uniform.

## EASY RENOVATION

If a step-by-step pruning job is too much work, then simply cut the entire shrub rose to the ground with a power saw. This should be done in late winter or very early spring, before the buds on the plant open. The rose will then throw new shoots (usually prolifically) and the gardener should identify the three to seven strongest ones and prune off the others to form the new and improved framework. A shrub rose on

its own rootstock can be cut flush to the ground with no ill effects. The beginning gardener can find out if the rose is growing on its own roots by checking for a bud union (see illustration, page 54). If no bud union exists, then the rose is on its own roots and can be cut heavily. If a bud union exists, then the rose is probably growing on a grafted rootstock; do not cut this rose to the ground but, rather, prune as described in the previous section.

The heavily pruned rose will continue to throw new shoots in its efforts to turn into a garden monster again. Some of these will have to be pruned out or dug up to share with other gardeners. Persevere with your plan for the rose, and use a sharp shovel to shear off any unwanted shoots. In a few seasons, once the top growth is as large proportionally as the roots, the production of new shoots will slow to a normal rate.

## TENDER HYBRID ROSES

RENOVATING LARGE-FLOWERED ROSES IN A cold climate is usually an easy job. "Simply wait until it dies and then replace it" is one classic bit of advice for gardeners, and all too often replacing becomes an annual chore. But by planting these roses deeply, we have been able to sustain them, winter after winter. Our pruning is routine and seasonal rather than for renovation.

In the fall, we prune our rose canes back to 12-inch stubs. This height marks the plants' locations and helps them hold snow cover throughout the winter. Because they are not protected with mounds of mulch, screens of burlap or any other strategy, the canes invariably die. In the spring, we cut the dead stubs flush with the ground. This is the extent of our pruning.

If you are struggling to keep large-flowered roses from being winter-killed, try the approach that has worked for us. Dig up your tender roses and replant them with the bud union 6 inches below the soil line. The ideal time to replant is right after the first hard frost or when the rose foliage can be easily plucked from the cane without tugging. Roses are one of the few plants in a cold climate that will tolerate a late October planting without serious winter damage.

Given that deep planting will help tender roses survive, our challenge is not to keep the plants alive but to encourage copious blooming year after year. Mulching and regular feeding are critical to reaching this goal. One fertilizer that has become a staple in our feeding program is manure tea. You can brew a wonderful brown "tea" in a few minutes by plopping a cloth sack filled with whatever manure is available—we use chicken manure—into a 5-gallon pail of water. We pour this liquid around our roses every week all summer long. (Tea made from compost or a fish emulsion fertilizer purchased at a garden center can also be used.)

Until you try feeding with manure tea, you will not believe what a difference it can make. The plants will often be larger and glossier and will produce more flowers. We are not concerned about our roses producing late-summer growth that might be winter-killed, because we prune our tender roses back to 12-inch canes each fall. So we feed the plants generously and enjoy the summer flowers.

## CLIMBING ROSES

### HARDY TYPES

The hardy "Explorer" rose series (bred in Ottawa, Canada) contains several varieties that can be trained into climbing roses. The advantage of these roses in harsh climates is that they do not require winter protection—the wrapping, burying or other arcane survival techniques necessary with hybrid tea climbers. Left unpruned, "Explorer" roses form wonderful bushes. They reward growers with a heavy flush of June blooms and they continue to flower lightly and sporadically throughout the summer. Trained up against arbors or fences, these roses put flight to the myth that northern gardeners can't grow a climbing rose. To be fair, these roses do not grow or bloom heavily all summer in the habit of a climbing tea rose, but then again, they do not die either. Easily reaching a height of 10

# HOW TO TRAIN NEW HARDY CLIMBING ROSES

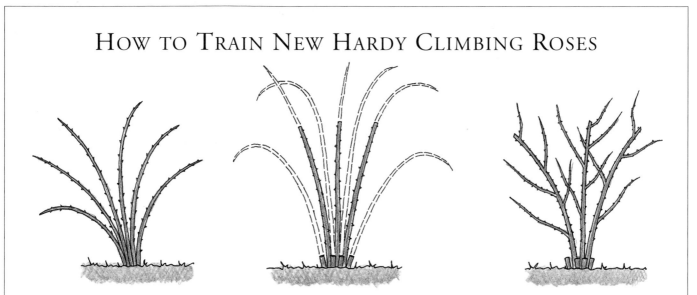

*Training a climbing rose is a three-year undertaking. In the first year, allow the plant to grow unpruned and unsupported (top left). In the spring of the second year, prune out all but three to five of the strongest canes. Remove about 6 inches from the tips of these (top center). Tie the canes to a support or weave the tips through a trellis. Side shoots will emerge from these canes (top right).*

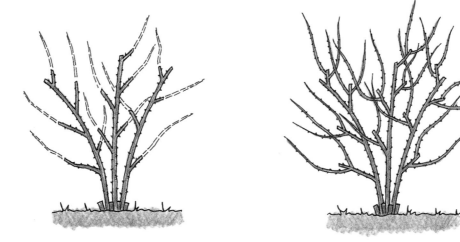

*In the spring of the third year, cut back the side shoots, or laterals, by half their length (above left). The rose will then develop strong new flower-bearing laterals (above right). Climbing roses become large, woody plants and need a sturdy, well-anchored trellis for support.*

feet, they deserve a spot in the northerly garden. The best climbers of the "Explorer" series are 'John Cabot' and 'William Baffin'. 'Jens Munk' has also been trained to climb by some brave gardeners who do not mind its wicked thorns.

Training roses to climb makes good use of vertical space, but it does not necessarily produce the most prolific bloomers. Climbing roses trained horizontally will flower along the length of the cane, while untrained canes growing vertically will tend to flower only at the tips and not along the length of the cane.

## TENDER CLIMBING TYPES

Hybrid climbing roses are a finicky lot in cold-climate gardens. Often, they simply lack the vigor to survive harsh winters, despite whatever protection the gardener might provide. Sometimes penetrating cold will kill the top of a hybrid climber but not the roots. New growth may appear in spring, lush and roselike in every characteristic but one—it does not flower. The usual explanation is that the hybrid variety is dead and only the rootstock remains vital. Examine the base of this flowerless plant. If all the stalks are suckers coming from below the bud union, it is a rootstock rose. Don't waste a season trying to coax it to bloom.

## RENOVATION OF CLIMBING ROSES

Renovation techniques for climbing roses—tender or hardy—are similar to those for shrub roses. The first step is to prune out any dead wood. You may need a long-handled tool known as a lopper to trim out these old stalks because they are often too large for the bite of a small hand pruner. Climbing roses that achieve a ripe old age can be very woody. After all dead wood has been removed, you may want to wait one season to evaluate the new growth. Mulching and fertilizing will encourage these new shoots.

The next task is to identify the main branches, or leaders, of the plant. Cut these leaders back to leave only vigorous new shoots—the largest are the most vigorous. Some of the shoots may have dead tips—victims of the winter. Prune these tips back to live wood.

Encouraging new growth is the overall objective in renovating, since climbing roses flower only on new growth. For this reason, cut all flowering laterals back to 6 inches. (A flowering lateral is any branch that supported flowers in the previous growing season; it is easily identified by the presence of rose hips or drying flowers.) Pruning encourages new growth, so cutting back laterals will force the rose to throw many new flowering branches.

The final step in renovation is to train new stems to fill in the gaps left by the removal of older, unproductive branches. Bend and tie the stems onto their trellis or support so they will grow in the desired di-

rection. New canes growing above the bud union (even if the bud union is underground) may also eventually produce flowers. Encourage new canes by choosing the largest ones and tying them to the trellis as well as pruning out the smaller, weaker canes.

The few hybrid tea climbers I have tried in my gardens have not survived as climbing roses, but we have an interesting result from one that was planted deeply. It top-kills every year, and we treat it as an herbaceous perennial ground cover rose. In the meantime, I shall keep looking for that mythical, hardy, everblooming, fragrant climbing rose for the northerly garden.

Rose gardeners should keep in mind that the microclimate of a favorable site can mean the difference between life and death to a climbing hybrid tea or other tender rose. Find the warmest, sunniest, breeze-free site and try to grow that tender climbing tea rose you admire. At worst, a few dollars will be wasted. At best, a very desirable plant will grace the garden, bring-

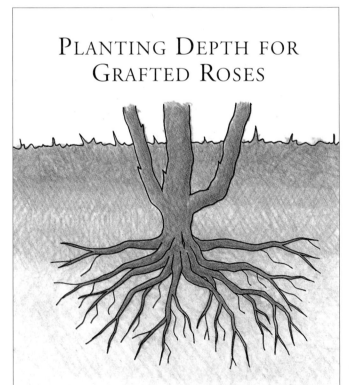

## PLANTING DEPTH FOR GRAFTED ROSES

*In cold climates such as USDA zone 4, grafted roses should be planted with their bud union 6 inches below the soil line.*

## RENOVATING A CLIMBING ROSE

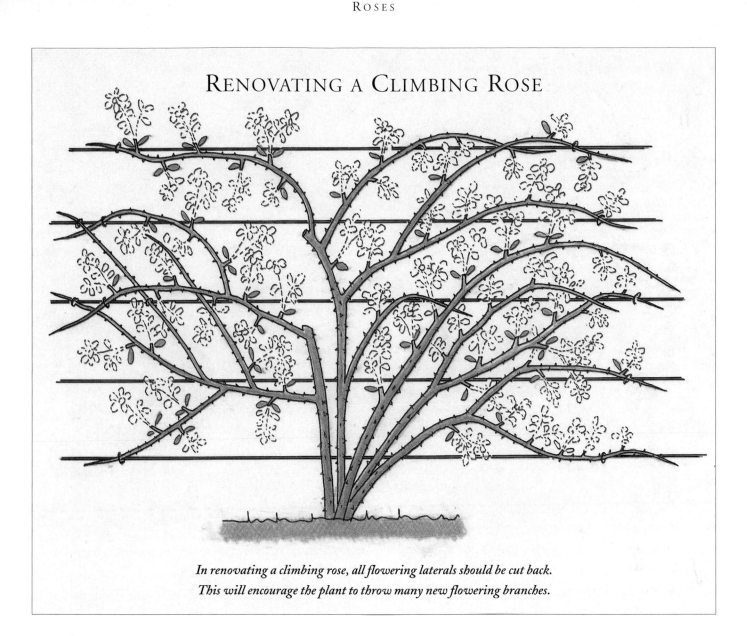

*In renovating a climbing rose, all flowering laterals should be cut back.*
*This will encourage the plant to throw many new flowering branches.*

ing a rare and fragrant delight to still, midsummer nights.

# PLANTING GRAFTED ROSES

MANY GARDENING BOOKS ADVISE WITH great assurance how deep to plant a grafted rose bush. In England and areas with a moderate climate, the usual recommendation is to plant so the bud union (where the rootstock and the scionwood join) is at soil level. For colder regions, experts often advise planting so the bud union is 1 inch below soil level. Unfortu-

nately, in cold-climate areas, this second bit of advice is often dead wrong, and many rose bushes are killed because of it.

At our Simple Gifts Farm in Ontario, grafted roses are planted with their bud unions 6 inches below the soil line. This may sound heretical compared with traditional advice, but our large-flowered roses—grandifloras, multifloras and hybrid tea roses—have survived in our gardens this way since 1987 (if you do not count the rose crushed by a bulldozer) with no winter protection. And with a consistent soil fertility program, we have not seen a loss of blooms over the years. Our garden is in USDA zone 4, where winter temperatures commonly drop to −30 degrees F. Neighbors regularly lose their carefully protected rose bushes, while ours survive with little coddling.

## COMBATING SUCKERS AND BLACK SPOT

ONE OF THE SIDE BENEFITS OF DEEP planting is that the roots of these grafted roses are not likely to send up suckers or wild canes, which sap the strength of any plant yet do not compensate the gardener with blooms. Remember, it is the scionwood grafted to the roots that bears the flowers. The roots only provide the vigor for the tops.

If your roses are planted at a more conventional depth, you will likely face the chore of eliminating these uninvited shoots. They can easily be eliminated with a claw hammer—but not by hitting them. First, ease soil away from the rootstock to expose the sucker. Then, as if the shoot were a nail, slide the claw around it, as close to the root as possible. With a firm twist, pull the offending growth off the root. (With a little practice, you can rip off these shoots without having to ease away any soil.) Although it sounds like a painful approach, ripping the shoots off does not hurt the main stems.

Merely pruning the sucker, instead of pulling it off, will encourage it to regrow and multiply. Eliminating suckers as soon as they sprout means you won't have to deal with them later on.

Identifying rootstock suckers can be a problem. The conventional advice of five leaves for a rose and seven leaves for a sucker is not reliable. Rootstock suckers are simply different from the main plant. They may have smaller leaves, the leaves may be shinier and, indeed, they may have a different number of leaflets, but their single most distinguishing characteristic is their points of origin. Suckers grow from the roots, from below the union onto which the scionwood is grafted. Tracing a stem back to the roots will conclusively differentiate a sucker from a cane.

If sucker growth is extensive, then a two-step renovation plan is necessary. Begin by cutting off the main suckers about 12 inches above the soil line. Then reach for the claw hammer and rip each sucker from the roots.

My roses have never been seriously troubled by black spot, although this bacterial ailment has terrorized other neighborhood gardens. We see a little bit of it in the fall but not enough to defoliate any plant or create an unsightly mess of yellow leaves. I used to think I was a superior sort of gardener until I read that Christopher Lloyd (English nurseryman, writer, gardener and owner of the sumptuous estate Great Dixter) was also raising roses free of black spot. He ascribed this healthy condition to the mulch applied to his rose beds. I, too, mulch all my beds, so it may well be that mulch, itself, has a dampening effect on the formation and growth of the bacteria. While I still prefer the superior gardener argument, mulching roses just may be more important to controlling black spot than a lofty sense of self-worth.

## CREATING NEW ROSES FROM OLD

PROPAGATING ROSES ENSURES THAT A favorite plant will not be lost. Even if a rose under renovation dies precipitously, a young plant will be available to take its place. Propagation is not difficult. There are three methods that work best in the home garden: rooting tip cuttings, digging up shoots and, with species or nonhybrid roses, starting seed. There is another method of rose propagation—grafting—but it is tricky and unnecessary, given the other options. (Books on rose grafting are available in the horticultural reference section of any good library—the technique will provide enough roses for the largest estate.)

### TIP CUTTINGS

Tip cuttings are the easiest way to perpetuate large-flowered roses. A tip cutting will produce a plant genetically similar to the original. The key with cuttings is to take them at the right time. If a cutting is too green (taken too early) or too woody (taken too late), it will be less likely to root and survive.

Taking tip cuttings is, perhaps, the ultimate test of a gardener's fortitude and singleness of purpose, because the best time to take a cutting coincides with the flowering of the rose. When a rose begins to bloom, the shoot supporting the bloom is ready for harvest. The true test of readiness is the "popping" sound a thorn makes when it is broken off its shoot. If the thorn bends, it is too green; if it fights back, it is too woody and not worth rooting. (Taking thorns off cuttings is a wonderful idea anyway—who needs the aggravation of constant pricking while working with them?) If you wait a week or two for the rose to finish blooming, the tip growth will harden and will be less likely to root. So for every cutting that is to be rooted, a rose bloom will have to be enjoyed in the house instead of in the garden.

Put this cutting in a glass of water to root. (Adding a slip of English ivy or willow to the water will help as each exudes a root-promoting hormone.) You can also root the cutting with the method described in Chapter Two and illustrated on page 33. This pot-in-pot approach works just as well for roses as the professional misting systems employed in our nursery.

Starting a rose from a tip cutting means that the plant will grow on its own roots. In theory, it will not perform as well as if it were on a more vigorous rootstock. However, that has not been the case in our gardens. We get quite acceptable production from roses that grow on their own roots.

## DIGGING SHOOTS

Roses that grow on their own roots, including bush-type hybrids and nonhybrid species, can be propagated by separating some of the roots and a viable shoot from a mother plant. (This technique does not work on grafted roses.) Ideally, this should be done in the early spring or fall when the rose has no leaves, because the transplant is less likely to become dehydrated.

Use a spade to sever a shoot with a generous amount of roots and soil. Make sure the roots and shoot do not dry out. Replant the roots as quickly as possible and water them thoroughly. The mother plant is not likely to be damaged by the shoot removal process, as long as a number of healthy roots remain undisturbed in the ground.

Moving a shoot during warmer weather demands a slightly different approach. The objective is to prevent the plant from losing more water than its newly severed roots can provide. The first step is to spray the plant, both the tops and the undersides of the leaves, with an antidesiccant wax (available at most garden centers). This will reduce moisture loss and keep the leaves turgid (a fancy horticultural term for not wilting). Working very early in the morning or on a cloudy day will increase the chances of a successful transplant. (If the day is rainy, the antidesiccant, which is sometimes also called an antitranspirant, will not dry. So move the plant and apply the spray as soon as the rain stops.)

Meanwhile, dig a large hole (twice the width of the roots) and fill it with water. While the water is draining, cut away the rose shoot and roots from the mother plant. Plant the shoot at the same depth it had been growing. Fill in the hole and water the shoot again. On sandy soil, soak the plant daily or every second day until new growth starts. If the soil base is clay, water more moderately but keep the ground damp.

Sometimes, on a garden visit, your host may offer you a rose shoot from a plant you have admired, even if the plant is not dormant. Accept the gift graciously, hurry home and proceed with the instructions above.

## STARTING FROM SEED

Species or nonhybrid roses, such as *Rosa rugosa*, can be started from seed. Rose seed is found in the round pods or hips that form after a plant has flowered. The seeds are ripe when the color of the rose hip fades and the skin starts to wrinkle; the seeds will be brown. Sow the seeds in the fall and treat them as you would the seeds of any other perennial (see Chapter Two, page 27, for detailed instructions on seed germination).

CHAPTER FIVE

# EVERGREEN SHRUBS

*"All theory, dear friend, is grey, but the golden
tree of actual life springs ever green."*

J.W. VON GOETHE (1749-1832)
***Studierzimmer (translation)***

SMALL CONIFERS, PARTICULARLY OF THE SPRUCE, PINE and cedar families, are the joy of the northern gardener's winter. Their compact lines and deep green or blue-green needles provide welcome color during the dormant season. At times, however, these plantings can fall victim to their own success. They can grow from endearing little shrubs into tall and unruly creatures, overshadowing other ornamentals or even the house they were intended to enhance.

In other landscapes, these evergreens may languish because of encroaching shade from maturing trees. A lack of sun can cause evergreen shrubs to become tall and shapeless and can kill the growth in the center of the plant. These shrubs may also face risks from the careless application of herbicides and even from dogs digging or looking for a convenient bathroom. Fortunately, it is not difficult to address these problems and to create conditions in which small conifers can thrive.

If an evergreen has grown much too large, the best approach may be

*Small conifers add texture and contrasting tones to both summer and winter landscapes.*

to remove it and replace it with another species of a more suitable size and shape. Don't put in a younger, smaller version of the same plant. Large, aggressive evergreens simply do not belong in small gardens. You may have to go to a specialty nursery that carries various dwarf species, but plants that mature to an appropriate size can certainly be found.

Among the many wonderful choices are dwarf pines, such as *Pinus strobus* 'Nana', which reaches only about 3 feet in height, and *Pinus strobus* 'Pendula' or *Pinus cembra* 'Nana', which reach about 6 feet in height. Perhaps the queen of the dwarf evergreens is the globe blue spruce, *Picea pungens* 'Glauca Globosa', which grows to a height of about 3 feet.

While you are looking for the perfect specimen to fit a particular spot in the garden, you can use a few renovation techniques that will tame most evergreens that have gotten out of control. These methods will en-

courage a natural growth form yet help alleviate OES, or Overgrown Evergreen Syndrome.

## RENOVATION PRUNING

BEFORE UNDERTAKING ANY RENOVATION pruning project, a gardener should understand that evergreen shrubs can have two kinds of buds along their branches—juvenile and mature. Successful renovation pruning depends on the existence of juvenile buds. Without exception, only the juvenile buds will sprout and form new growth if you prune off the tip, or growing point, of a branch. On most conifers, the buds mature within two years of being formed, unless the branch is pruned and the buds are stimulated to grow.

Buds form and mature as branches grow. The farther a bud is from the growing point, or tip, of a

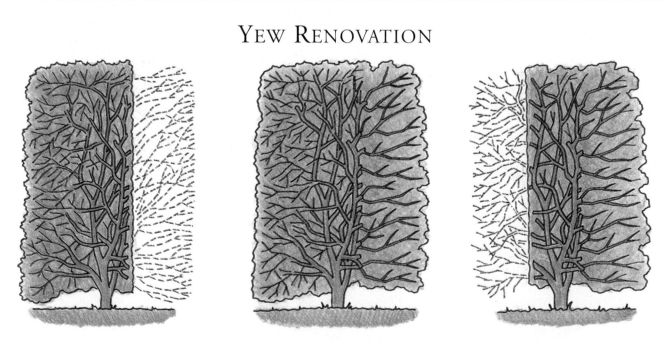

## YEW RENOVATION

*Yews retain their juvenile buds along the entire length of a branch. So a yew can be cut back to its central trunk and it will still resprout. An overgrown yew can be renovated in two stages. First, cut the branches on one side back to the main stems (left). This will allow new growth to emerge (center). Wait a year or two, then follow the same technique on the other side (right).*

*Low-growing evergreens combined with dwarf and standard varieties offers a visual transition from lawn to woods.*

branch, the more likely it is to be mature. Unfortunately, you cannot tell the difference between mature and juvenile buds by looking. In fact, you can rarely see the buds at all—they are only bumps beneath the bark—so you must be careful about how much of any branch you remove. If you cut a branch back beyond the juvenile buds, you will create dead spots, or brown holes, where the mature buds will not regenerate.

The primary exception to the rule of bud maturity within two years is yews (*Taxus* species), which retain their juvenile buds along the entire length of a branch. A 200-year-old yew can be cut back to its central trunk and will still resprout, so individual yews or entire hedges can be completely rejuvenated.

Yews are also more shade-tolerant than other evergreens. If you are planning a hedge adjacent to tall, overshadowing trees or in an area that will eventually be overshadowed, yew is a prudent alternative to cedar (*Thuja* species). Even if it is well cared for, a cedar hedge will eventually suffer if nearby trees reduce its sunlight. The shade will kill sections in the hedge, and these dead zones cannot be rejuvenated. Yews are slower growing and more expensive than cedar, but they make a more attractive and longer-lived hedge.

## PRUNING DEPTH

IF YOU EXAMINE MOST LARGE, UPRIGHT evergreen shrubs, you may be surprised to see that the layer of green needles does not extend very far into the interior of the plant. The green needles are confined to the outer 6 to 8 inches, and the remaining branches are largely devoid of foliage. There is simply

# COMMON MISTAKES OF CEDAR HEDGE TRIMMING

*Given the many opportunities for error in pruning a long hedge,*
*careful planning and the use of reliable guides, such as a line level, are advisable.*

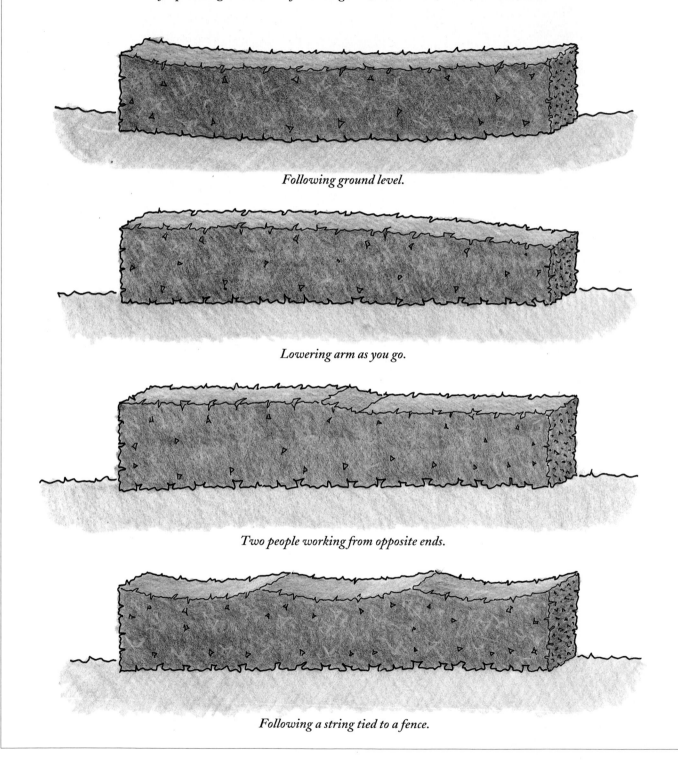

*Following ground level.*

*Lowering arm as you go.*

*Two people working from opposite ends.*

*Following a string tied to a fence.*

not enough light penetrating the interior to maintain good leaf growth. When you prune, you should stay outside of this dead zone, or you will expose defoliated areas that cannot be rejuvenated. How far you can cut back, then, depends on the depth of the green foliage. As a rule, never cut away more than about one-third of the living foliage on the side of an evergreen.

When trimming the top of a shrub, also take into account the height of the plant. If the plant is an upright evergreen with a flat needle structure, such as a cedar or juniper (*Juniperus* species), you can cut back the height by almost one-third without any permanent damage. Removing this much of the evergreen will leave the top flat and a dead zone exposed. However, if the top of the plant remains above most people's view, the open center will not be an eyesore. Over time, the flat-topped appearance can be softened by lightly pruning the tips of the upper branches. (Remove only about ½ inch of growth.) This will stimulate the juvenile buds to produce new growth and close in the top of the plant.

Such an extensive pruning, that is, cutting off about one-third, should only be undertaken once during the life of a flat-needled evergreen. It is not likely that the shrub can be trimmed any shorter than it was during the first extensive pruning without creating a permanent dead zone at the top because there will be no more juvenile buds to produce new growth. For example, if a hedge has grown to a height of 10 feet, you can cut it back to 7 feet and still stimulate new growth from the remaining branches near the top. If the hedge then grows to a height of 11 feet, you can only safely cut it back to about 7½ feet, since there will still be juvenile buds at this height to fill in the top.

If the hedge plant is an upright but less dense species, such as a pine (*Pinus* species), you can cut back the top without killing the plant, but it will not be very attractive. Pines and other long-needled evergreens do not fill in; they continue to look as if they received a 1950s brush cut. If you have overpruned a pine or inherited one that has been topped, you can try to soften its appearance by training a branch as a new leader and letting it start to form top growth, but this is a slow and uncertain process.

Long-needled shrubs simply do not respond well to being dramatically shortened. They must be pruned annually and lightly to keep their height in check. Usually, if a pine or other long-needled shrub outgrows its location, you might as well cut it down and plant a different species.

Ground-hugging, horizontal evergreens used as foundation plantings, such as *Juniperus horizontalis* 'Blue Chip' or *Juniperus procumbens* 'Nana', can be shaped with a different strategy. If you want to make the plant appear smaller and neater, you can lift up the top branches and remove some of the branches underneath. The upper branches will shroud the cuts left by the pruning and the plant will look significantly smaller.

Heavily cutting back a small ornamental evergreen will not necessarily kill it immediately (evergreens can survive a surprising amount of abuse), but it may spoil the plant's appearance and it will certainly affect the design and beauty of the garden. However, mature evergreens that are severely topped or pruned may die within a few years, especially if they are subject to other stresses. Successful pruning is a gradual process that should begin when a plant is young, not after it has matured.

# Curing Brown Spots

WHEN AN AREA OF FOLIAGE ON THE SIDE of an evergreen dies, the resulting dead or brown spots can spoil the entire appearance of the plant. And, depending on the evergreen species, there may not be much you can do about it. However, there are a couple of tricks that are worth trying.

If the dead spot is very small, it does not matter where on the plant it occurs. Gently prune the live growth around the edge of the dead spot, taking off

## PRUNING GROUND-HUGGING EVERGREENS

*Lift up the top branches and remove some of the branches underneath.*
*The upper branches will shroud the cuts left by the pruning, and the plant will look significantly smaller.*

about ½ inch of foliage. This will force new growth that may gradually cover over the brown spot, particularly if the plant is adequately fed and watered.

If the area of dead foliage is large and near the bottom of the plant, there is an interesting technique for improving the plant's appearance. The first step is to trim off the dead branches and needles, right to the center of the plant. The resulting hole will seem huge, but the next step is to plant another identical but much smaller evergreen right next to the cavity. As the new plant grows, it will cover the hole with a bit of trompe l'oeil landscape magic. This trick is especially useful for large cedar hedges that have lost the bottom of their "skirts" because of dog damage or the careless use of a weed trimmer.

For small or medium-sized holes, either at the top or bottom of a plant, there is another worthwhile technique. First, remove the branches that are devoid of live foliage. Then, pull any nearby living branches toward the center of the dead spot and tie them together with string. This leaves a smaller hole. Give the tips of the branches a light pruning (cutting back about ½ inch) to encourage new growth, which will fill in the

hole. Leave the string around the branches for several seasons. Eventually, the branches will be trained to stay in place without being tied.

If a large dead spot occurs high on an evergreen from, for instance, winter dieback or physical damage, there is not much that can be done. The gardener has two choices: learn to live with the damage or replace the plant.

## RELOCATING AN EVERGREEN

WITH A PATIENT APPROACH AND A STRONG back, most evergreens can be successfully moved. However, the uncertainties increase with the size of the plant. Long-needled conifers, such as spruce (*Picea* species) and pine (*Pinus* species), are quite a challenge if they are taller than 3 feet, because both species resent having their roots disturbed. (Speci-

*Shearing evergreens annually stimulates outer growth*
*and keeps the plants proportional to their setting.*

*The dusky blue tones of spruce accent the greens of deciduous foliage and the floral display of many perennials.*

mens less than 2 feet tall can be moved with much less risk.) With any evergreen, you not only need to move as many roots as possible, but you also must try to keep them undisturbed. This means that, even with a small evergreen, the rootball—the roots and the surrounding soil—is likely to be quite large and heavy.

The first step when moving an evergreen is to dig a trench at least 2 feet deep around the plant at the drip line, or outer edge of the branches. Then, begin digging under the roots. The best way to do this is to turn the shovel upside down and pull soil away from the bottom of the rootball. When the entire rootball is undercut, carefully work a tarp underneath the plant. You may have to tilt and jockey the evergreen and get help from a few other hands, but stay at it—patience will pay off. The more carefully you handle the rootball, the greater the chances that the transplant will succeed. A rootball 3 feet in diameter will weigh about 100 to 150 pounds. Larger specimens will have root-

balls that weigh several hundred pounds and may take the entire neighborhood to move.

If the shrub is only being moved across the yard, it may not be necessary to tie a tarp around the rootball. But all hands should be careful when lifting or dragging the plant to its new home. If the plant is being moved some distance, especially if it is being trucked or trailered, completely secure a tarp around the rootball with string or heavy cord. Otherwise, the roots may crack when they are jostled.

If the plant is very large, you may want to call in a professional tree mover. An expert can back a "clamshell" machine right up to the plant and dig it out of the ground in one simple operation. Because the clamshell makes a hole the same size every time, the new hole will perfectly accommodate the rootball. This assures good soil contact for the rootball and an almost guaranteed transplant operation. Then you will need to make sure the plant has adequate water.

Evergreens can be moved anytime the ground is not frozen, except in late fall. Late fall plantings do not give the roots enough time to reestablish themselves before the ground freezes. Without adequate root establishment, the plant is less likely to survive the winter. The intense heat of summer is probably the second worst time to transplant. However, the chances of success are greatly enhanced if you spray the evergreen's needles with an antidesiccant before you start the move. In fact, applying an antidesiccant is helpful in any transplanting job, regardless of the season. Once an evergreen is settled in its new home, keep it well watered until it is established.

# EVERGREEN CARE

MOST EVERGREENS DEMAND FULL SUNLIGHT. In certain landscapes, the maturing trees or shrubs can create a "creeping" problem that the gardener may not immediately notice. A garden that started in full sun may, over time, become quite shady. This gradual encroachment can lead to branches dying in the center of a shrub and can cause spindly new growth. The solution to this problem is to replace the sun-loving evergreens with those that tolerate shade, such as yews (*Taxus* species). No amount of pruning will solve problems created by a lack of sunlight.

As with most plants, evergreens depend on food and water to maintain strong growth and disease resistance. An annual spring feeding of a balanced fertilizer or several shovels full of compost will provide the necessary nutrients. Deep waterings, especially during hot spells, are also critical for long-term survival. Thoroughly irrigate established evergreens once a week using a soaker hose or a trickle from a regular hose.

Dogs can pose a serious problem for evergreens, especially if they dig around foundation plantings or use the base of a prized specimen as a bathroom. Male dogs can ruin a shrub in a matter of months. The best hope for alleviating urine damage is to saturate the area around the shrub with water in an attempt to flush the urinary nitrogen out of the root zone.

Preventing the damage is easier than reversing it. One approach is to apply two or three coats of antidesiccant to the branches, from dog height down to the ground. This will cover the foliage with a protective layer of wax, which will need to be renewed in two to three months.

The digging habit is also easier to prevent than reverse. In our experience, dog repellents do not work if a dog has already begun digging in a bed. Dogs must be trained from the time they are puppies to stay out of an area.

An elaborate but effective way of protecting plants from even the most stubborn dog is to rope off the garden with a strand of electric wire. (Some communities have regulations governing the use and placement of electric fences, so you should check with your municipal officials before installing one.) There are various fence setups sold specifically for pet control, but the cheapest and most reliable units are usually found in farm-supply stores.

Sometimes a single encounter with an electrified wire is all it takes to discourage a dog. We had a golden retriever that would not keep out of my alpine bulb garden, no matter how much he was scolded. He thought he had as much right to dig in the bed as I did. I ran a strand of wire around the bed and he soon made its acquaintance. The zing sent him skipping across the garden on his tiptoes, and needless to say, he never ventured near the alpine garden again.

Another problem for evergreen shrubs can be herbicides. Unfortunately, once the damage is apparent, there is little a gardener can do except replace the plant or prune out the dead areas. As an emergency response, you can try flooding the soil around the shrub with water in hopes of washing the chemicals out of the root zone. The best solution is to refrain from using herbicides in the first place.

CHAPTER SIX

# $\mathcal{V}$INES

*"Fill every beaker up, my men, pour*
*Forth the cheering wine:*
*There's life and strength in every drop*
*—thanksgiving to the vine!"*

A.G. GREENE (1802-1868)
**The Baron's Last Banquet**

OR ALL PRACTICAL GARDENING PURPOSES, VINES ARE simple plants to grow. Most species require only an annual spring feeding and the removal of any dead wood to keep them healthy and attractive. Although there are many species with wonderfully varied foliage and flowers, all vines climb and support themselves in one of two ways, either by twining or by sending out adhesive discs, or hold-fasts, that cling to a building or trellis. Either type of vine will respond the same way to renovation pruning, but knowing how it climbs becomes important when you want to dislodge a vine and lower it to the ground.

If a vine uses hold-fasts, pulling it away from a wall may damage the wall itself. Instead, cut the vine away, leaving the hold-fasts attached to the wall. If the wall is brick or stone, wire brushing or sandblasting will

*With their dense foliage and climbing habit, vines like clematis screen out the world and provide serenity.*

remove the vine remnants. If the structure is wood and requires repainting, hold-fasts must be tediously scraped off. Once the hold-fasts are removed, prune the vine to within several feet of the ground. Without this heavy pruning, the vine will have too much top growth to reestablish itself easily on the wall. Pruning any vine should be done during the dormant season or very early in the spring before full growth has begun.

Twining vines that are growing on a trellis are easy to remove from a wall. Simply unfasten the trellis and lay it and the vine on the ground. There is no need to separate the vine from its scaffold. It will endure being on the ground for several weeks, if necessary, while the wall is being repainted or repaired.

Do not be reluctant to prune any vine heavily while it is dormant. Vines can be cut back to main branches without any lasting damage. In fact, pruning stimulates an amazing amount of new growth. In no time, the plant will re-cover the wall.

Before planting a vine, it is usually a good idea to prune off one-third to one-half of its top growth. This will force the vine to put out new and abundant shoots that will be better able than the old growth to cling to a wall or throw tendrils for climbing. With food and water, most vines grow very quickly.

Once they are established, vines only need pruning to remove dead wood and to discipline them away from windows, vent pipes and other forbidden zones.

## CLEMATIS

### (*Clematis* species)

Clematis is one of the most beloved of all vines and one of the most misunderstood. But a few simple rules make growing this twining vine relatively easy. First, grow clematis in full sun—the leaves of this plant love the heat. Second, shade the shallow tender roots by mulching. Third, remember to feed and water the plants—they profit from huge amounts of compost in spring. The better the soil, the better the plant growth.

When planting, bury the clematis rootball 2 inches deep. This is slightly deeper than it is likely to be growing in the nursery pot, but deeper planting will help the vine throw more shoots and reduce the incidence of clematis wilt. A vigorous plant is less likely to be attacked by disease or insects.

In the spring, before the leaves emerge, prune off all the dead branches. Some clematis will be dead right to the ground, while others will be green and pliable for several feet up. There is some risk that a gardener may inadvertently cut off old wood thinking that it is dead. To avoid this pruning mistake, give the wood a slight twist before you cut it. If it breaks easily, it is dead. You can also identify dead wood by scraping the bark with a hand pruner. If the underlying tissue is brown, the branch is dead; if it is green, it is alive.

I have had customers tell me they add peat moss to the soil because clematis love acidic soils. Other customers tell me they add wood ashes to the soil because clematis love alkaline soils. I simply smile and tell them to make the soil as rich as possible. Adding lots of compost, bone meal, balanced fertilizers and water is a reliable recipe for success. If you enrich the soil, a bit of peat or wood ashes won't hurt, and everybody can believe they know the secret to growing clematis.

## PORCELAIN BERRY

### (*Ampelopsis brevipedunculata*)

In full sun or partial shade, this vine, which supports itself with twining tendrils, is fast-growing and will quickly cover a trellis or other garden structure. Its foliage is attractive and similar to that of a grape vine, but it is primarily grown for the wonderful display of blue berries that cover the entire vine late into the fall. If grown in a moderately fertile soil and protected from whistling winter winds, this vine will do very well in the garden.

Pruning is quite easy: remove any dead wood or invasive tendrils from eaves troughs or windows. If limited space is a concern, the vine can be cut back quite hard in the spring. Cut each branch emanating from the main stem back to a length of a few inches, leaving only several buds. These buds will sprout and form a very thick columnar vine. Repeat this hard pruning every spring in a small garden.

## BITTERSWEET

### (*Celastrus scandens*)

Bittersweet is an aggressive twining vine that will climb almost any structure or nearby tree. Females growing near a male pollinator will produce wonderful coral-red berries in the fall, so in a landscape setting, you will likely want one plant of each gender. If you are buying plants, choose ones that are at least three years old. By that age, females will be easy to identify in the fall by their berries or in the spring by the remains of berries still clinging to the vines; males will be apparent by their lack of berries. There are a few plants in this species with bisexual flowers, but these are not generally available in the nursery trade. Several named varieties have better flowering habits than the species and, although hard to find, they may be worth the search. 'Indian Brave' (male form) and 'Indian Maiden' (female form) are two that provide an impressive display.

Bittersweet requires no pruning, training or maintenance other than removing the odd dead branch in the spring. It grows well in the sun or shade and is perfect for covering a spot where nothing else will grow. A shovel or two of compost in the spring will keep it quite happy for the whole season.

## TRUMPET VINE

### (*Campsis radicans*)

Trumpet vine is a ferociously rampant climber in sunny or very lightly shaded gardens. In fertile soil, its exuberance is hard to control, and the multitude of seedlings it produces can make it more of a noxious weed than a garden friend. However, it is redeemed by its abundant beautiful scarlet flowers, which it bears from midsummer to early autumn. A yellow variety, 'Flava', is also available.

When planting, cut the vine back to 12 inches to promote good bottom branching and enable this twining vine to fan out on whatever supports are provided. Any structure needs to be sturdy, because this woody, rampant vine becomes quite heavy by midseason.

To renovate the plant, cut back every branch and leave only two to three buds on the stubs. The plant will thank you with prolific displays of new growth and flowers. Pruning should be done in early spring, because the vine flowers on its current season's growth.

Trumpet vine may top-kill in a particularly bad winter, but it will send up a flush of new growth from its roots. Regardless of the weather, it is one of the last vines to leaf out in the spring; impatient gardeners have to curb their impulse to declare it dead. Once it leafs out, it will grow with great energy.

## ENGLISH IVY

### (*Hedera helix*)

I have tried many species of English ivy at our nursery; with the odd exception, I cannot get them to survive the winter. A friend who gardens only a few miles away uses them as luxuriant ground covers but notes that their top growth is killed if they poke their heads above the snow. If you live north of zone 5 and are intent on growing English ivy, the varieties 'Baltica', 'Wilson' and 'Thorndale' are the hardiest. Grow them in just about any soil, but do not feed them heavily. The lush growth produced by heavy fertilizing will not survive the winter. In northerly gardens, English ivy is better grown as a ground cover than a vine.

English ivy will grow in the sun, but it is particularly adaptable to the shade. It clings with hold-fasts and easily mounts walls of wood or brick. College buildings across central North America sport acres of its shiny leaves.

Where winters are harsh, the weather will prune these vines, leaving gardeners to remove only dead material. In milder areas, disciplinary pruning should be done in the spring.

## BOSTON IVY

### (*Parthenocissus tricuspidata*)

Understanding that these vigorous vines were originally found in moist woodland soils will help gardeners successfully site Boston ivy. It thrives in soil with lots of organic matter, adequate water and shade, although surprisingly, it will tolerate urban air and some drought.

Boston ivy uses hold-fasts to cement itself to a wall, so try to ensure that any vertical surface is in good condition before the vine is planted at its base. Pruning every year is almost mandatory. Uncontrolled, it can clog downspouts and cover windows. Rigorous pruning is not going to hurt this vine, so feel free to cut where necessary to control its growth.

Though it is rated as hardy in USDA zone 4, Boston ivy is badly burned or killed back by winter temperatures that plummet to −30 degrees F. Some plants will persist for several years, but eventually they will die in a particularly cold, windy winter.

## VIRGINIA CREEPER

### (*Parthenocissus quinquefolia*)

This North American native has never met a wall it doesn't like. It is self-clinging with tendrils and hold-fasts, so no support is necessary. It will quickly find its way to the top of whatever wall or trellis it faces. In fact, without annual pruning, it can cause structural damage. Its tendrils work into cracks and openings where they continue to probe and expand.

This vine does not require renovation or selective

pruning. It can be cut to the ground and will happily resprout to chase the sky. It cannot be hurt by any known pruning methods.

The best-known variety, 'Engelmannii', has a brilliant red fall color, which is spectacular across the entire wall of a building.

## JAPANESE WISTERIA

### (*Wisteria floribunda*)

If cold hardiness is a prime consideration, this species of wisteria is the one to choose. It can be reliably planted in USDA zone 4. As an experiment, I grew one plant for four years in an unprotected site where it was exposed to late-spring frosts, full winter winds and intense cold. One year, it died back to the ground, but it produced new shoots in the spring and soon recolonized its wire fence.

The Chinese wisteria (*Wisteria sinensis*) is not reliable in cold winter areas. Oddly enough, the Japanese and the Chinese species twine in opposite directions, so they are easy to tell apart. Japanese wisteria has a clockwise twining habit, while the Chinese wisteria twines counter-clockwise.

Although Japanese wisteria is quite hardy, a protected site will allow it to develop its flower buds more fully, as they are sensitive to late-spring frost. In full bloom, wisteria can be spectacular, producing clusters of pendulous flowers up to 24 inches long. Grafted varieties produce more abundant and more reliably shaped flowers than plants raised from seed.

In its native habitat, Japanese wisteria grows on moist soils in semishaded streamside thickets or on the edges of woodlands. Trying to grow this plant on dry clay soils will only prove frustrating.

If a wisteria lacks vigor and is reluctant to flower or if it has become unruly, improving its environment is the first step you should take in the process of renovation. Add organic matter to its root zone to create a rich soil with good moisture-retaining quality. Wiste-

# RENOVATION OF WISTERIA

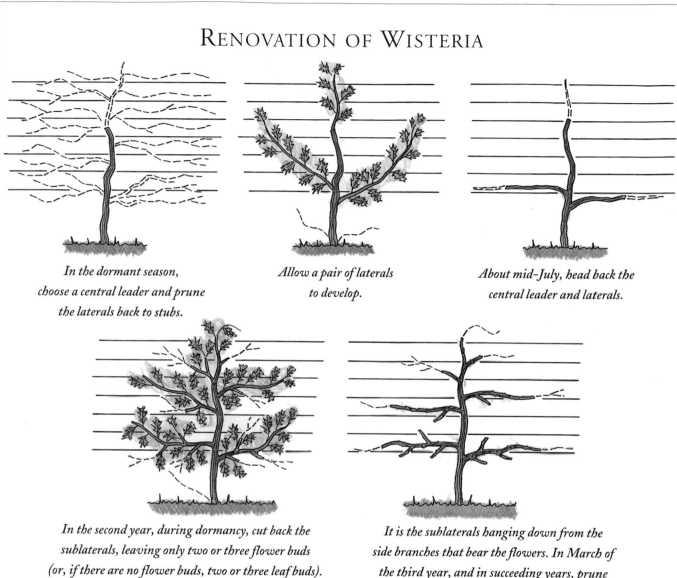

*In the dormant season,
choose a central leader and prune
the laterals back to stubs.*

*Allow a pair of laterals
to develop.*

*About mid-July, head back the
central leader and laterals.*

*In the second year, during dormancy, cut back the
sublaterals, leaving only two or three flower buds
(or, if there are no flower buds, two or three leaf buds).
By May or June, lush new growth will appear.*

*It is the sublaterals hanging down from the
side branches that bear the flowers. In March of
the third year, and in succeeding years, prune
back the central leader and the laterals.*

ria favors a partially shaded location. In full sun, it will thrive only if attentively watered.

Pruning to restore shape and productivity is not difficult. During the dormant season, choose the branches that will grow to form the main framework. Select a central leader and the appropriate side branches to form an espalier shape (as shown in the illustration), or prune out all the side branches and leave only the multiple leaders to form a fan shape. Of the two forms, an espalier will be easier to prune and maintain and will give more flowers than a fan shape. While it may seem drastic to remove the branches and leave only a basic framework, it is a pruning strategy that will virtually guarantee blooms. From the basic framework, the remaining side shoots or laterals will quickly begin to grow in the spring. In about mid- to late July, cut back these laterals to leave only one-third of their new growth. This will force the laterals to produce side shoots or sublaterals. It is along this growth that blooms are produced.

The following spring, while the plant is still dormant, cut back all the sublaterals to leave only two or

*In full bloom, wisteria lends an ageless grace to any setting.*

three flower buds. The flower buds are easily distinguished from the leaf buds because they are fatter. If there are no flower buds on a particular sublateral, cut it back to two or three leaf buds. This system will stimulate blooming within a few years unless the plant is top-killed by a very cold winter.

## HONEYSUCKLE

### (*Lonicera* species)

Honeysuckles, both bush and vine forms, are easy to grow and require little renovation other than pruning off the occasional dead branch. However, if you enjoy pruning or want to keep your plant a particular size or shape, you can certainly remove old branches without impeding vigor. As much as one-third of the old wood can be taken out each year. New growth will quickly replace whatever you prune away.

The bush forms of honeysuckle flower more profusely when planted in full sun, but the vines do equally well in sun or shade. However, like clematis, the vines prefer their foliage in the sun and their roots shaded or mulched. Bark chips, leaves or grass clippings make excellent mulch and will help the plant thrive instead of merely survive.

Pruning or transplanting should be done in the dormant season. Once established, honeysuckle vines are fast-growing. They require a trellis around which to twine themselves.

The old-fashioned vining honeysuckle (*Lonicera periclymenum*) bears fragrant flowers and so do its many varieties. However, the more modern vining hybrid *Lonicera* x *brownii*, called 'Dropmore Scarlet', has no bouquet at all. While this information will not affect your renovation strategy, it may explain why your nose is not drawn to the modern red honeysuckle flower.

## SILVER LACE VINE

### (*Polygonum aubertii*)

This native of western China, Tibet and Tadzhikistan is a fast, rampant grower that is hardy in our USDA zone 4 gardens in all but the coldest winters. Its rapid growth and tightly spaced leaves make it ideal for creating dense shade over trellised walls or patio coverings. Flowering in late summer and early fall, when many other ornamentals have passed their peak, its fragrant white blossoms create a special garden event.

Equally at home in full sun or partial sun, the vine can grow 25 feet or more in a single season. In a good site, it is capable of producing hundreds of seedlings, which must be assiduously weeded out each spring. Sometimes called "mile-a-minute vine," silver lace will outgrow most competitors on a trellis, so planting it with other vining species is not recommended.

Other than removing dead wood, no renovation is required with this twining vine. However, some gardeners make a habit of pruning it back quite hard every spring. While not necessary, this may appeal to those with an urge to cut or prune something annually.

If silver lace is killed back to the ground during a particularly harsh winter, do not be concerned. It will resprout from its roots to reclaim its fence or trellis.

## CLIMBING HYDRANGEA

### (*Hydrangea petiolaris*)

Once established, this climbing vine virtually takes care of itself. Simply feed it, water it and keep grass away from its base, ideally with a heavy mulch. Then sit back and enjoy its multiple blooms.

As soon as its roots are well anchored, a young climbing hydrangea will take off and rapidly cover the side of a building. Clinging tenaciously with hold-

fasts, it vigorously resists removal. Its slow then suddenly rampant growth is aptly described by the old garden rhyme: "It sleeps, it creeps, it leaps."

Climbing hydrangea enjoys sun or partial shade and is tolerant of a wide range of soils, but it prefers neutral to slightly acidic soil rich in organic material. You can amend sandy or heavy clay soils each year with large amounts of compost. Although a climbing hydrangea does not need routine pruning, it will respond with bursts of growth if it is heavily cut back. If a vine needs to be removed so that the wall behind it can be painted or repaired, cut the plant back to its main trunk during the dormant season.

## DUTCHMAN'S-PIPE

### (*Aristolochia durior*)

Renovation pruning of Dutchman's-pipe is usually more a matter of keeping this huge-leaved twining vine in check than of stimulating new growth. However, pinching the stems in the spring will encourage branching if you are trying to shape the vine to a particular site or climbing structure. If the vine becomes too massive, cut it back heavily in late winter. In some areas, penetrating cold will occasionally prune the vine back to its roots each winter, but the plant will spring back with the return of warm weather. Simply cut away the dead wood to make room for new growth.

Native to moist woodlands, Dutchman's-pipe thrives in shady locations where few other vines venture. It will establish in hot sunny spots, too, if its soil is kept moist. The vine's growth is rampant, and it will quickly cover a large area of the garden or a wall, but because it requires support, it can be easily controlled. Its branch tips will begin to flop down once they extend beyond the trellis.

Dutchman's-pipe is named for its flowers, which are shaped like little meerschaum pipes. Unfortunately, the purplish brown blossoms are not fragrant and are usually hidden among the big heart-shaped leaves.

# CHAPTER SEVEN

# TREES

*"Poems are made by fools like me,*
*But only God can make a tree"*

A.J. KILMER (1886-1918)
*Trees*

TIME GIVES TREES THEIR LOFTY STATURE IN THE landscape. Slowly, over the years, their spreading form creates an attractive environment for birds, animals and humans. In summer, their shade can be cool and inviting. In fall, their foliage can set the world aflame with tones of yellow, orange and red. From one season to the next, the angular lines of even a single tree add visual richness to a yard and increase the value of any home.

Despite their prominence, trees are often taken for granted. Slow growing and apparently indifferent to neglect, they are sometimes ignored until we finally notice dramatic evidence of illness, in the form of dying branches or falling leaves. Trees are not invulnerable, they are simply slow to show their wounds. Preserving their health is an investment not only in our own future but in that of succeeding generations. If a mature tree dies, it cannot be replaced in one person's lifetime. For our own sake, trees deserve all the care we can give them.

*With time, trees such as this maple achieve a lofty stature in the landscape.*

# BASIC CARE

AN UNDERSTANDING OF SOME BASIC BIOLOGY is useful when considering the renovation or repair of an ailing tree. Trees are, by nature, forest dwellers. They are part of a living community, a balanced ecosystem in which they are born, grow and die. In dying, they return their nutrients to the soil. Among trees, other plants, animals, insects and even microorganisms, there exists an interdependence too subtle for any casual observer to grasp.

Trees thrive in their forest community but we want them to live on our front lawn. We take away their forest soil enriched with generations of leaf mold, and we substitute backfill and sand. We add competition for water and nutrients by planting grass. If the grass doesn't grow because the tree, doing what it does best, shades the ground, we cut off limbs to let more light through. We use herbicides and fungicides to kill any biodiversity that may thrive on the lawn. We pave over part of the tree's roots to make a sidewalk, cut off another part for the driveway and disturb the rest for sewer and water lines or for a home addition. We chop off lower limbs and plaster on a petroleum goop to seal the wounds. Then we drive spikes into the wood to hold up our toys, ropes and hammocks. We use this lonely giant of the forest for our own designs but sometimes ignore its needs for food and water. And yet we wonder why it is bothered by insects or lacks vigor. We wonder why its bark splits or its branches die. The answers to these questions take us back to the basics of preventive care.

Providing food and water for trees is the first step to ensuring that they can survive in the sometimes hostile environment of our backyard. Water can be particularly important. A large tree will use several hundred gallons of water a day during the heat of summer. Replacing some of this will keep the ground moister and the tree's roots cooler and healthier. At least once a week, put a hose at the base of the tree and let the water steadily trickle out overnight. Rains may fall during the summer, of course, but in some settings, much of the water lands on pavement and other hard surfaces and is channeled into storm drains and away from tree roots.

Trees in a forest obtain many of their nutrients from the decaying leaves that blanket the soil. When you rake up leaves, you take away this food. You can compensate for this nutrient loss by composting the leaves and spreading the compost back under the trees. If this is not practical, apply a commercial fertilizer to provide the minerals that trees need for energy and growth. Balanced tree fertilizers with a 10-10-10 formulation are available in the spring at any garden center.

# WOUNDS AND REGENERATION

NATURE CAN BE HARD ON TREES. VIOLENT winds or the weight of winter ice can tear branches and split the trunks of even strong and towering trees. People, too, with misguided construction equipment, vehicles or garden tools, can damage innocent trunks and branches. Add to these the injuries caused by rabbits and mice feeding on bark during the winter and you have the potential for tree trauma from the ground up.

The most common response to tree damage is for a concerned gardener to rush out and paint the wounded area with some concoction sold to promote healing. Gardeners in ancient Japan mixed rat dung into their healing compounds. One English arborist included lime in his particular remedy. Modern salves use other ingredients, but their value is the same as that of their counterparts in centuries passed. Wound dressings have no positive effect. In fact, they can cause harm. In a covered wound, bacteria remain active and potentially damaging long after they would have expired if the injury were open to the air.

*Flowering dogwoods and redbuds light up the late-spring woods.*

Tree biologists studying discoloration and decay in forest trees have found that trees do not heal their wounds; they wall them off and do not need a coating of sealant to help them. As Dr. Alex Shigo, who worked for the U.S. Forest Service for more than 25 years, found, trees create chemical boundaries to contain a wound and keep infection from moving through the rest of their system. If fungi or bacteria invade the wound, there is a biological race to see if the tree is healthy enough to seal off the area before the invaders can spread. The competition becomes a complex interaction in which the tree calls upon its energy reserves to combat the pathogens. The healthier the tree, the more successfully it can compete.

Trees store energy in living cells. If a tree has to compartmentalize or wall off an area that contains living cells, the energy in those cells is lost to the tree. If a limb is cut off, the energy in those cells is also lost. These energy reserves are required to fuel the biochemical processes of compartmentalization and decay resistance. Energy is also needed to begin the process of growth in the spring. When energy is lost due to the removal of branches, the tree can literally starve to death.

As Dr. Shigo found, dying limbs can be the result of a tree trying to save itself. The question to ask is, "What caused the tree to give up on the limb and wall it off instead of fighting the invader farther out on the branch?" The spread of a pathogen is not necessarily the cause of decline, but rather a symptom of weakness.

Similarly, Dr. Shigo's research indicated, ants are not a cause of decay. While their passageways are found in decayed areas, ants require airy, dry surroundings to survive. The fact is, ants probably retard the spread of decay by their fastidious housekeeping.

# TREE PRUNING CUTS

*Correct pruning is close to but does not cut the branch collar, which enables a tree to wall itself off from disease.*

*Branch collar*

*Wrong cut*          *Wrong cut*          *Right cut*

A tree's response to aging, like its reaction to injury, also differs from that of humans and animals. Aging in humans can be measured by the ratio of cell breakdown to cell regeneration. As the body takes longer to regenerate, the rate of aging increases. But trees do not regenerate areas that have been wounded. Aging in trees is determined by comparing how much wood with living cells is being walled off because of injury or illness with how much wood with living cells is being created. When a tree can no longer produce more areas of living cells than it is losing to walled-off areas, it begins to die. A tree must grow to live.

In a mature tree (one with a large mass of wood to maintain), the balance is nearly equal between energy produced and energy consumed. If a living limb is removed, the loss of energy stored in its cells may mean the difference between a mature tree living for several seasons and it plunging into irreversible decline.

Stress on a tree causes 90 percent of its problems, and most stress is caused by people. Misguided grass trimmers or "whipper snippers" are one of the worst sources of injury. The whirling nylon string can bruise or slash through young bark in a matter of seconds.

Bruising at the bottom of a mature tree can interfere with the flow of nutrients and translate into falling foliage or dead limbs. Instead of whipper snipping close to a tree, try removing the grass in a 3- to 5-foot-diameter circle around the trunk and covering the area with 3 to 4 inches of mulch. Not only will this suppress grass and eliminate the need for trimming, it will also preserve moisture in the soil and insulate the tree's roots against intense summer heat.

Tree stress is also commonly associated with construction projects. Soil becomes compacted, which poses a risk to roots, trunks can be bumped by heavy equipment, and roots can be disturbed by excavation. Concentrations of herbicide or fertilizer on a new lawn can also damage trees, as can excessive pruning. By the time the stress is evident, it is often too late to save the tree.

There is a faint hope for trees with bark injuries caused by machinery or nibbling rodents. An old practice involves packing wet peat moss completely around the wound and covering it with black plastic. Tying this plastic bandage (a garbage bag is fine) tightly to the trunk and leaving it undisturbed for six months may allow some of the bark to regenerate. Apply the poultice as soon as you notice any damage. The earlier the treatment, the better the chances of success.

Injuries from cats are another matter. They can be prevented quite easily. Being independent and sometimes contrary creatures, cats often like to use your newly planted tree to sharpen their claws. Fortunately for your trees, most cats are fastidious and don't like to get their paws messy, so you can discourage their scratching with horticultural glue and masking tape. Put the masking tape around the target tree (or trees) in a spiral fashion so the trunk resembles a barber's pole. Then smear the tape with Tanglefoot or some other nondrying horticultural sticky stuff. After about two years, the tape will be cracked and hardened and can easily be removed. By then, the cats should have found another target. If not, repeat this process. Do not apply wound dressing to areas of the bark that cats have already damaged.

# PRUNING

THERE MAY COME A DAY WHEN SOME PRUNING is necessary for the health of a tree or to keep a branch from damaging your house or utility wires. Pruning can also be important for stimulating new growth and promoting production on fruit trees. Even if you hire someone for the job, it is useful to understand what kinds of cuts may be used and the effect they may have on the tree. While this information is included here because of the specialized needs of trees, pruning is just as important for shrubs and houseplants. Understanding pruning helps a gardener restore a tree and maintain it in optimum health.

There are two different kinds of pruning cuts: thinning cuts and heading cuts. Each is appropriate for achieving specific results.

A thinning cut removes an entire branch back to where it started as a bud. There will be no new growth after a thinning cut is made. Thinning cuts are used to remove dead or broken branches or branches that are crossing or chafing. They are also used to remove unwanted shoots or old wood from the base of a bush or shrub.

Heading cuts remove only part of a branch. Different kinds of heading cuts remove different lengths of branch. Shearing, for example, removes only the relatively soft outer tips of all the branches, while topping removes a certain amount of wood (but never the entire branch). Whether on a geranium or a young apple tree, heading cuts stimulate new growth. But they are rarely advisable on large branches of mature trees. The cut will result in either a dead stub—a possible invitation for decay—or it will encourage a lot of rapid, weak, vertical growths called "water shoots" or "water sprouts."

A badly pruned tree may be loaded with water shoots on the stubs of its branches. Whether you did the original overpruning or not, you can return the tree to a healthy form by being patient and restrained. Do not remove all the shoots at once. They will only resprout, in many cases in larger numbers than before. Instead, allow the shoots to grow out, then identify the largest, thickest and fastest-growing of each group. This is the sprout to keep. Do not prune the rest out immediately (the tree has produced them because it needs their energy). Thin them gradually, removing one or two sprouts each year from every stub. The best sprouts will form new branches, and the tree will regrow into an attractive specimen.

If a pruning job involves making a thinning cut and removing an entire branch, study the limb before you pick up the saw. Find the section of the branch adjacent to the trunk—the section larger in diameter than the rest of the branch. This swollen area, which can extend out at least 1 to 4 inches from the trunk, is called the "branch collar." It is within the branch collar that a tree is best able to wall itself off from the rest of the limb. Cutting a limb flush with the trunk may appeal

# PROPER BRANCH REMOVAL

*Two common errors in removing a dead branch: failing to make an undercut (left) and cutting into the branch collar (right).*

*Failing to make an under-cut will cause the limb to rip down the trunk.*

*Sawing too close to the tree will injure the branch collar and invite disease.*

*Removing a long, heavy limb may require cutting the branch twice to keep it from tearing away from the tree. Make the initial cut a foot or more from the base of the branch. Undercut the branch first, then finish the cut from above, as shown at right. Then trim back to (but not into) the branch collar.*

to some beginning pruners as a smooth and neat resolution to an ailing or unwanted limb. But such a cut removes the tree's natural disease barrier, along with the branch. When you cut, leave the branch collar.

When a limb has died, the tree has already walled off the injured area. But for safety, you may want to remove the limb before it falls. Follow the same strategy for dead branches as you would for live ones: cut close to the trunk but avoid trimming off the branch collar.

The same goes for a branch that has been torn from a tree by high winds, ice or some other trauma. If you make a smooth cut clear of the branch collar, the tree should wall off the injury. If the branch has been entirely torn off and strips of bark are pulled from the trunk, it is advisable to remove any jagged edges of bark and leave a smooth wound. This is called "scribing." It is never done when removing a healthy branch. Using a chisel and hammer, carefully tap your way around the tear, cutting the bark back to where it joins the trunk tightly. Make all your cuts as shallow as possible to avoid damaging living tissue. Round the edge of the wound, but do not cut away any firmly attached bark just to obtain a circular shape. At one time, arborists advised trimming the edges of the wound to make a diamond pattern, but experiments have not shown this to be of any value. Rounding and minimizing the area of bark removed seem to offer the best chance for recovery.

Any tree pruning job carries some risks for the pruner. To keep the work as safe as possible, consider these guidelines before you start:

• If the work is high enough to require a ladder, it is too high to undertake unless you are a trained arborist. Consider hiring a professional.

• Avoid working near power lines.

• Wear protective equipment for your head, feet, hands and, especially, eyes.

• Use properly sharpened tools that are in good working order.

• Do not operate a chain saw over your head; you will have no control over it.

• Use great care when cutting or trimming trees that have been toppled or twisted by a storm. They are under a great deal of stress and may kick back or snap unpredictably. Consider hiring a professional.

• Avoid cutting major limbs at the end of the day, when you are tired. It is always the last job that is the most dangerous.

# RENOVATING CONIFERS

CONE-BEARING EVERGREENS, SUCH AS PINES, spruces, hemlocks and arborvitae, form an important element in many landscapes, both as hedges or informal screens and as individual specimens. They offer color and wildlife habitat throughout the year, particularly in the winter when the foliage on deciduous trees has turned brown and fallen from the branches.

The cone-bearing evergreens are more ancient and genetically simpler than most deciduous trees. Few have any flowers in the ordinary horticultural sense of the word, and they are largely wind-pollinated, unlike deciduous trees, which do flower and depend, in large measure, on insects for pollination.

But when it comes to pruning, the same rules apply to both deciduous and coniferous trees. Conifers may weep a more visible sap or pitch—that is to be expected and not something you should try to control. Do not clean off the pitch or paint the cut to stop the bleeding. If the pruning is properly done, the tree will stanch its own wounds.

One of the unique challenges for conifers is that misguided souls are forever cutting their tops off to keep the trees from getting taller. This makes about as much sense as cutting off someone's head so he can fit through a doorway. A topped tree is likely to go into decline and may be killed by the first serious shock it faces—anything from a drought to a severe winter. (Unlike deciduous trees and many long-needled conifers, yews and other flat-needled conifers, such as junipers and cedars, can be safely cut back, or topped, by almost a third of their height. Once one of these conifers has been shortened, the remaining upper branches can be lightly pruned back with heading cuts. Trimming the branches will soften the flat-topped appearance of the tree, and it will stimulate new growth from dormant juvenile buds along the branches, which will further round off the top.)

If you find yourself the owner of a topped tree, ensure that it has adequate nutrition and water. Keep grass and power trimmers away from its roots, and perhaps it will endure. If, despite your efforts, the tree declines, you might as well remove the tree and give it a decent burial.

Removing a tree that is "too tall" for a particular spot is better than topping it and watching it slowly decline. Some years ago, we had a problem at our farm with an overgrown Manitoba maple. This maple is a weed tree and its roots can destroy the foundation of an old home, but in the summer, we deeply appreciated the shade it cast across the front of our house. For several years we considered taking the tree down. Then a vicious ice storm made the decision for us by splitting the trunk in half. We missed the shade for several summers, but as our newly planted Ohio buckeyes mature and throw enough shade to sit under, I wish we had cut down the maple years before.

Evergreens, too, cast heavy shade and, unfortunately, this quality is often held against them. Many gardeners cut off the bottom limbs of evergreens so more light will reach the ground and grass will have a chance to get established. To sacrifice the sweeping lower limbs of an evergreen in an attempt to please the great North American god of lawns seems a misplaced devotion. Better to respect the tree and keep it healthy. Grass may not even grow under an evergreen with its branches cut. (You can use a photography light meter to measure whether an area has enough light to support grass growth. If the meter measures less than 300 footcandles, the shade is too dense.) Try growing shade-tolerant ground covers, or mulch the area and enjoy the tree's natural form.

Even under deciduous trees, the soil and light conditions may not be conducive to other plants. However, you may succeed in establishing hardy, shade-loving perennials or spring bulbs (which flower before the tree has fully leafed out) by improving the soil between a few of the major roots. Remove some of the soil with a hand tool, being careful not to disrupt small feeder roots, and mix the soil in a 50:50 ratio with compost. The plants will find adequate nutrition in the soil mix and, if kept watered, will be able to compete with the tree.

# RENOVATING APPLE, PLUM, CHERRY AND PEAR TREES

FRUIT TREES THAT HAVE BEEN NEGLECTED for years or improperly pruned may flower profusely but bear small, malformed fruits that are easy targets for insects and disease. If the tree is still within its most productive years (younger than about 45 years old), it can be returned to full fruiting with some pampering and a gradual systematic pruning. If the tree is more than 45 or 50 years old, it will often be more rewarding to remove it and plant a young tree.

Before you get out your pruning shears, start giving the tree attentive care. You will want to reduce any stress that may be sapping its ability to bear sound fruit. Water the tree and remove grass from around its trunk. Replace the grass with a 4- or 5-foot-diameter circle of mulch that is 3 or 4 inches deep. Feed the tree with a

*A single well-pruned, well-tended apple tree can provide bushels of fruit.*

# Pruning Fruit Trees

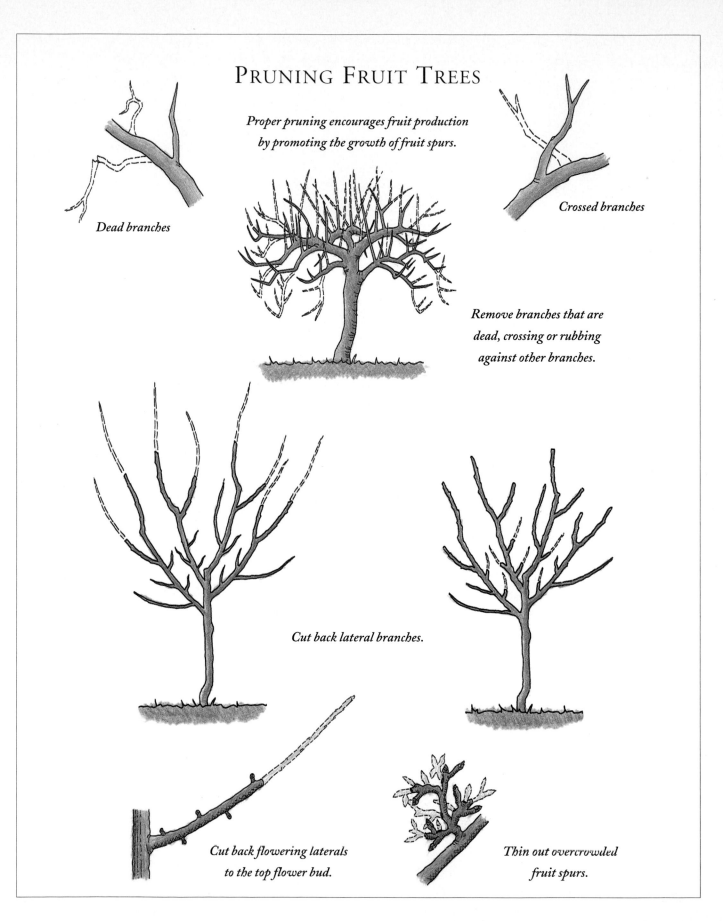

*Proper pruning encourages fruit production
by promoting the growth of fruit spurs.*

*Dead branches*

*Crossed branches*

*Remove branches that are
dead, crossing or rubbing
against other branches.*

*Cut back lateral branches.*

*Cut back flowering laterals
to the top flower bud.*

*Thin out overcrowded
fruit spurs.*

balanced fertilizer applied in the late fall or very early spring (late October or early April in my area). A late fall feeding, when the tree is dormant, is actually preferable, because the nutrients are within the root zone all winter and available in the spring as the tree makes a burst of early-season growth.

Once you have boosted the tree's vigor, you can take some steps toward a thorough renewal pruning. First, identify the dead branches. To simplify that job, mark them in the summer when the other limbs are in full leaf. Tie a piece of twine around each one or spray it with a bright-colored paint. Then, in late winter or early spring (the most appropriate time for pruning), remove all the branches you have marked. Follow the methods described earlier in this chapter. Make clean cuts that avoid sawing through the branch collar.

Old, neglected fruit trees may have a lot of dead wood in their crowns. Cutting away these decayed branches will enhance the growth of the living limbs by allowing them more space and light. It will also give you a better look at the tree's structure. This is important for the second stage of pruning—removing branches that are rubbing against or crossing other branches. Limit your first year's pruning to these dead and crossing or rubbing branches. In fact, you may have to spread the work over two years, depending on how many live branches are involved. A primary rule of pruning is never remove more than about 25 percent of the leaf surface of a fruit tree in a given year.

Renewal pruning is a gradual process. Trees need time to adjust. It is not possible to "fix" 25 years of neglect in a single growing season. Clean out the interior of the tree. Make sure that all remaining branches are healthy and growing well. Let three or four years pass before you consider removing any major branches. For many trees, there will be no reason to cut main branches. In other trees, you may want to remove some of these branches gradually, bringing the most productive section of the tree closer to the ground so the fruit will be easier to spray, thin and pick.

Once the tree has recovered from its renewal pruning and is being fed and watered properly, it should begin to bear larger and healthier fruit. At that point, the home orchardist may want to simply remove any crossing branches each March to maintain the tree's basic form and productivity.

Pruning can also be carried one step further. The yield of the tree can be increased through a fairly easy process of identifying lateral branches (those that shoot off from the side of a main branch) and not cutting these branches during spring pruning. By the following year, these uncut laterals will have produced long shoots, and there should be a number of flower buds on the older wood of each shoot. In that second spring, cut back this new lateral growth to the outermost flower bud on each branch. The remaining buds, farther down the branch, should open up and produce fruit for the current season.

The next pruning season, cut about half of these fruiting laterals to half their length. This will encourage the growth of fruiting spurs, which look like thick buds on short woody stems. Cut the rest of the laterals right back to the branch from which they originated, leaving only a 1-inch stub. In the next fruiting season, the spurs on the laterals that were cut to half their length will bear fruit, and new laterals will grow from the stubs on the other branches.

By following the procedures outlined above, you will have begun an annual pruning strategy. Every year, cut one-half of the laterals back to their originating branches and cut back the remaining laterals to half their length to produce fruit spurs. As the spurs mature, they will require thinning to encourage fewer, larger fruits. Take off the smallest spurs and those on the underside of a branch, which tend to be the least productive.

Renovation pruning is an ongoing chore, whether on a fruit tree, shade tree or conifer. Like tree growth itself, it is a process that is never finished. Yet the work is pleasant and the results can be endlessly rewarding.

CHAPTER EIGHT

# SMALL FRUITS

*"What beautiful fruit!*
*I love fruit when it's expensive."*

SIR A.W. PINERO (1855-1934)
***The Second Mrs. Tanqueray***

NOTHING EXCEEDS THE TASTE OF FRESHLY
picked, juicy red raspberries still warm from the sun,
heaped onto a bowl of vanilla ice cream. Unfortunately, the raspberry plants themselves are sometimes
less delightful. They can get ahead of a gardener who
neglects them and become a tangled, unproductive mess. A bit of ongoing maintenance will keep most brambles bearing heavily, but even if
they have been neglected, it is not difficult to bring raspberry brambles
and many other small-fruit plants back into full production. And the
rewards are worth the effort.

Small-fruit plants, such as raspberries, gooseberries, currants and
strawberries, have simple needs if they are to fruit and prosper in the garden. Without exception, they grow best in full sun. Planting them in a
shady spot is an invitation to lower yields, weaker stem and stalk growth
and some formidable diseases. Instead of trying to grow small fruits in an
inappropriate location, why not accept the limitations of the spot and
raise shade-tolerant plants instead?

*Small-fruit plants like raspberries have simple needs.*

Just as small fruits need full sun, they also need freedom from competition with weeds and grass. Grass in the strawberries or tall weeds around the base of berry bushes means less food and sunlight for the plants and fewer fruits for the grower's table. Attentive weeding or mulching is important to limit competition and keep fruit plants at their most productive.

Small-fruit bushes also need to be fed. Any suggestion that they can feed themselves by relying on their large root systems to scavenge for nutrients is a myth. If a plant is to earn its keep, especially in a small garden, it must bear the maximum amount of fruit possible each year. Maximum fruiting requires feeding and care from the gardener. (See Chapter Ten, page 126, for a general guide to plant nutrition.)

Fruit is mostly water. Commercial growers recognize this and provide irrigation. Home gardeners, too, must provide water to obtain large harvests. A strawberry is more than 90 percent water, and if the plants are not irrigated when the berries are bulking up, the fruit will be small and, perhaps, less flavorful.

# RASPBERRIES

THERE ARE FEW THINGS IN THE GARDEN SO discouraging as a patch of overgrown raspberries—masses of dead canes, thorns so thick they fight back, grass as tall as the fruiting canes and fruit so small it is hard to justify picking even the easily reached ones. There are several ways to address this problem: replace the canes, renovate the patch the hard way or renovate the patch the easy way. The approach you choose should be based on the funds and time available and your energy level. In the end, each system can create a strong and productive bed.

## REPLACEMENT

Replacement has its advantages. All canes can be easily and indiscriminately cut down with a lawn mower or weed whipper and the roots dug up with a tiller or garden fork. The ground, tilled and root-free,

can be double-dug and renovated into a fertile bed. Grass roots will be eliminated, and disease-free, high-yielding raspberry canes can be replanted. The resulting bed will be a joy to work with, and the fruiting canes will begin producing again the year after planting. (Without double-digging, there is very little sense in replacing the canes. You will be putting new canes into the same ground and watching the old problems recur. See Chapter Ten, page 123, for a description of double-digging.)

When planting new canes, place them on 24- to 36-inch centers. Commercial growers often set plants only 12 inches apart, but in a home garden, the added space will give the gardener time to train the canes and shape the beds while the plants are filling out.

Raspberries thrive in rich organic matter. Copious amounts of compost or composted manure should be added to the soil to increase organic levels; it is almost impossible to add too much.

Also consider installing a drip irrigation system (see Chapter One, page 15). Raspberries will greatly benefit from being watered when the fruit is starting to develop and plump up. Drip irrigation makes it very easy to get water to the roots of the plants at these critical times.

If more than one row is planted, the rows should be at least 6 feet apart. This allows rototillers, lawn mowers and people to move in between the rows without being attacked by the spreading canes. Cane plantings allowed to grow and spread to about a foot wide will reduce the width of the aisle from 6 feet to 5 feet within a few years.

## RENOVATION

### The Hard Way
Renovating canes the hard way involves identifying the plants to be left in a narrow row, then removing all others. As a rule, leave only the six strongest canes in every square foot of row. Removing the rest of the canes can be done by hand or by machine. If you use a tiller, cut all the undesired canes to the ground and remove them before tilling so they do not

# RASPBERRY REPLACEMENT

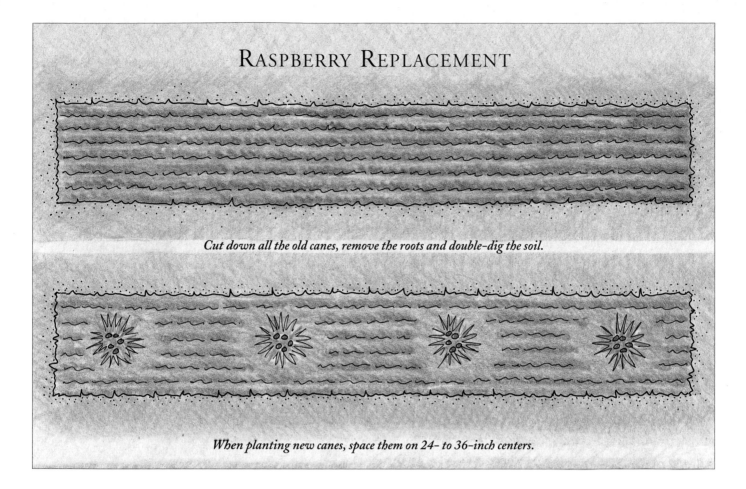

*Cut down all the old canes, remove the roots and double-dig the soil.*

*When planting new canes, space them on 24- to 36-inch centers.*

become wrapped around the tines of the machine. If you do the job by hand, trim the canes back a bit but leave enough stub to grab hold of so you can tug the unwanted canes out of the ground. Prune the remaining canes so that each plant is no more than about a foot wide. You want room to work between the rows without having your arms scratched to shreds by the thorns. In any case, long sleeves and a pair of stout leather gloves are essential apparel for raspberry renovation work.

Because this is a partial renovation and does not involve double-digging, weed roots will still maintain a strong hold in the beds. There are two ways to eliminate these established weeds—hand-pulling them or applying herbicides.

Hand-weeding throughout the summer will get rid of the unwanted weeds. Admittedly it is a chore, but it involves only time and effort—no toxic materials.

If you employ chemicals, follow the directions to the letter. Consult your local cooperative extension agent or garden-center authority to select an herbicide appropriate for the soil conditions and weeds found in your garden. Under no circumstances should you use a material that happens to be in your tool shed; some herbicides will kill the berry plants or, worse, will be absorbed by their roots and passed along to you through the fruit.

Deep mulches, unfortunately, will not stop established grasses. They will slow down new weeds, but they will also provide comfortable habitat for rodents to overwinter and feed on the bark of young canes.

### The Easy Way

Renovating raspberry patches the easy way involves the use of machinery, rather than a lot of hand-digging. Mow the patch to the ground using repeated passes with a lawn mower at its highest setting. This will leave a level area containing stubs of canes. Mark where you want the new rows to be, then run a tiller slowly and deeply over the stubble. Remove the canes

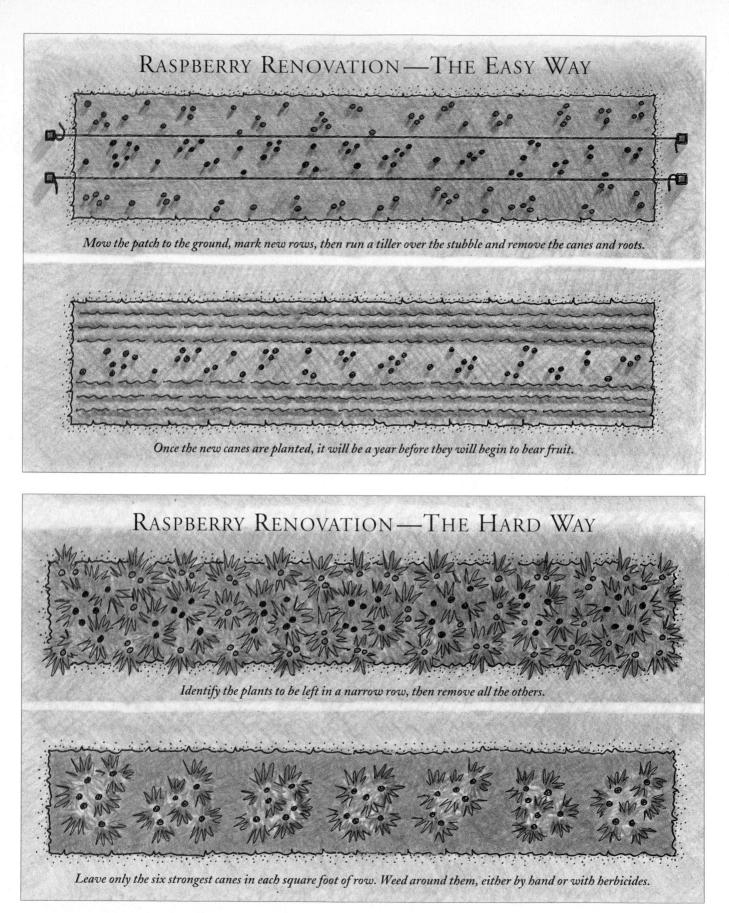

# RASPBERRY RENOVATION—THE EASY WAY

*Mow the patch to the ground, mark new rows, then run a tiller over the stubble and remove the canes and roots.*

*Once the new canes are planted, it will be a year before they will begin to bear fruit.*

# RASPBERRY RENOVATION—THE HARD WAY

*Identify the plants to be left in a narrow row, then remove all the others.*

*Leave only the six strongest canes in each square foot of row. Weed around them, either by hand or with herbicides.*

and roots thrown to the surface by the tiller. You can then weed in the rows. The more conscientiously you weed, the less competition the berries will have in future seasons. If the soil is dry, moisten it before weeding. You can then pull the roots out much more easily. (You can also use herbicides if that is your choice.) Without the canes in the way, you can use a small shovel or other hand tool to remove stubborn roots. Then set in the new canes. This method's only drawback is that a year of harvesting is lost; the advantage is that it is easy.

A corollary to the easy method is the super-easy method that I practiced for a few years on a large, wild raspberry patch beside our home. With our lawn mower at quite high a setting, I cut pathways into the huge patch to open it up for walking and harvesting. The paths improved air circulation and increased the amount of sunlight that was reaching the remaining plants; this, in turn, reduced disease problems. We were able to harvest raspberries with no weeding or digging. A simple mowing once or twice a year was sufficient. This is a wonderful technique in rural areas, but it is tremendously wasteful of space in an urban garden. Those with wild patches in rocky ground might consider cutting the paths with a weed whipper outfitted with a steel brush blade rather than with a mower.

## MAINTENANCE

Raspberries will do their part to put fresh fruit on the table; gardeners just have to do theirs. The most important ongoing task is to maintain no more than six canes in every square foot of patch. All others—the smallest and weakest—should be pruned out every spring. If the row is kept to a width of 1 foot, this pruning job will be easier. Maintaining that width is a job for either a sharp and continuously used hoe, a rototiller or—the lazy man's way—a lawn mower regularly run along the row to snip off new, wayward canes. Each system, if used properly, will keep young canes from spreading beyond the 1-foot bounds of the row.

Another maintenance task is to feed raspberries reg-

ularly. Compost, manure or a combination of bone and blood meal will work wonders. Two feedings—once in early spring just before the plants leaf out and once in early July—will keep the plants happy. Supplement these feedings with an application of manure tea when the plants are setting fruit. Also, attentively water the plants during fruit-set and while the berries are plumping up. Our canes are never tipped or top-pruned in any way; that is extra labor and it cuts off some berries. Harvest the berries regularly to keep ahead of the birds, which appreciate them as much as we do, even without vanilla ice cream.

# BLACK CURRANTS

RENOVATING A BLACK CURRANT BUSH IS A straightforward operation. As with many bush plants, the first step is to remove all dead or obviously very old wood. Remove any crossing branches or wood that is being rubbed by another branch. This initial renovation can be done anytime the plant is not in leaf (fall through late spring). New growth stimulated by the rigorous pruning will likely bear heavily the following year.

After this initial cleanup, renovation in the second year will proceed quite quickly and smoothly. Again the work should be done when the plant is not in leaf, and at least one-third of all old branches should be removed.

Recognizing old branches on black currants is not complicated, but the gardener needs to be observant. Old wood is darker in color than new wood. Darker is a relative term, and fine distinctions may be difficult to make when comparing the wood on two different plants or even branches on the same plant. Do not agonize over every cut. A little overpruning or underpruning will not damage this plant. If you take out about one-quarter to one-third of all the old branches, the plant should respond properly.

Two seasons of this pruning strategy should be enough to remove the oldest and least productive branches. In year three and afterward, remove only

# BLACK CURRANT RENOVATION AND PRUNING

*In the spring of the first year, remove all dead, crossing and rubbing branches.*

*If setting out a new plant, cut the laterals back to short stubs.*

*Allow a new plant to grow for one year without further pruning.*

*In the summer of the first year, the renovated plant will fruit on old wood.*

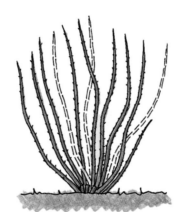

*In the spring of the second year, remove one-third of the oldest branches. Allow new branches to grow in.*

*In the summer of the second year, the bush will throw many new shoots.*

the oldest and worst-looking branches every dormant season. If this is done regularly (see illustration) the bush will soon begin to throw lots of new shoots, and you can start preparing to make the most delectable spread for toast—black currant jam.

Once the plants have been renovated, they need routine care and pruning to maintain good fruit production. Black currants fruit most prolifically on wood produced the previous summer, so you need to prune each year to stimulate the growth of this wood. The objective in pruning is to have a regular succession of strong, new shoots. This can be achieved by removing at least one-quarter to one-third of the old wood annually. Such harsh pruning must be done if the plant is to set fruit each year.

Black currants are not particularly fussy about their soil conditions, and while they prefer full sun, they will tolerate a lightly shaded location. They are greedy feeders, so larger than normal amounts of compost or fertilizer (two to three ounces of 10-10-10 fertilizer per plant in the spring) will greatly help both growth and fruiting.

It is also important to know that black currants bloom early in the spring, and their flowers can be quite susceptible to frost damage. (Because of their early bloom time, black currants should not be planted in a frost pocket or a particularly frost-prone area.) In cold areas beset by spring frosts, there are a couple of tricks that will sometimes delay flowering long enough to avoid frost damage. You can plant black currants on a north slope to reduce their exposure to the warm spring sun and thus retard blossoming, or you can keep the roots of the plant cool by packing snow around them. Either trick is worth trying. If the flowers are destroyed by frost, there will be no fruit.

## WHITE AND RED CURRANTS

WHITE AND RED CURRANTS HAVE IDENTICAL growth habits, so all comments about renovation apply to both plants. These currants are different from black currants in the way they fruit. White and red currant bushes bear fruit in clusters, some at the base of one-year shoots and the majority on spurs growing on older wood. To encourage these spurs, a good framework for the plant must be created and maintained. If a bush is renovated to a height and width of 5 to 6 feet and is bearing properly, it should produce between 8 and 10 pounds of fruit per plant.

White and red currants tolerate a wide range of soil conditions, except soggy, poorly drained ground. Their flowers are more tolerant of late frosts than black currant flowers, and they bear well in shady locations, although not as prolifically as in full sun. If a garden has few sunny locations, this is one fruiting bush that can still be rewarding.

An old or neglected currant bush is likely to be a mass of tangled branches—both old wood and new—growing in all directions. Deciding where to start renovating is half the battle. Luckily, the starting point is the same as for most woody shrubs: eliminate all dead, broken, crossing and rubbing branches. This general cleanup makes identifying the overall framework much easier.

The timing of fruit-bush renovation is identical to that of other shrubs: the work should be done during the dormant season when no leaves are on the plant. The steps described for gooseberry renovation and maintenance (see page 104) are also applicable to red and white currants.

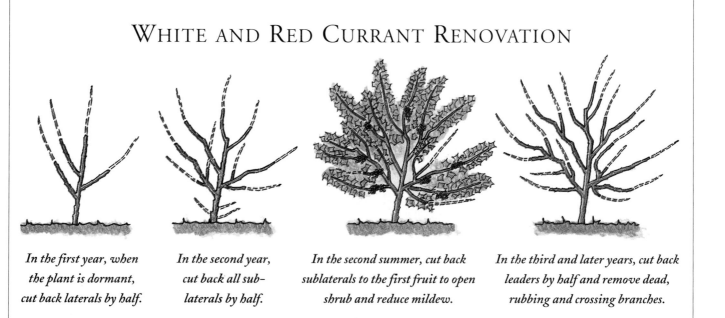

## WHITE AND RED CURRANT RENOVATION

*In the first year, when the plant is dormant, cut back laterals by half.*

*In the second year, cut back all sub-laterals by half.*

*In the second summer, cut back sublaterals to the first fruit to open shrub and reduce mildew.*

*In the third and later years, cut back leaders by half and remove dead, rubbing and crossing branches.*

# GOOSEBERRIES

AN OVERGROWN GOOSEBERRY BUSH CAN BRING tears to the eyes of the sensitive gardener—not because of nostalgia or grief for the loss of fruit, but because of the anticipated pain from having to prune this plant. Gooseberries fight back. Their thorns are forbidding, so stout gloves and long sleeves are a must for pruning.

A mature gooseberry is an imposing bush—it is often 5 to 6 feet wide and equally tall. It tolerates partial shade but does best in full sun where it will produce a wealth of fruit (6 to 8 pounds per year). Like the black and red currant, the gooseberry bears fruit on the base of new shoots but mostly on spurs of the previous year's growth. This means that mature but controlled growth is necessary to keep the plant healthy and bearing well. Restoring this plant is an easy, straightforward task as long as the gardener takes the thorns into account.

Begin renovating by removing all dead, broken, crossing and rubbing branches. This opens up the shrub and allows you to evaluate its framework. The gardener should then identify six to eight major supporting branches that are equally spaced around the plant. Once these branches are identified (mark them with ribbon or string), all other branches should be removed by cutting them out at ground level. The second step in the first-year renovation process is to cut all the leaders, or one-year-old branches, to one-half their length. This will promote new shoot growth farther back on the supporting branch.

The first summer after you begin renovating (July is ideal), shorten all the new growth so only five leaves remain on each shoot. This will force new lateral growth and prepare the plant to begin fruiting. A secondary benefit of pruning in July is that it removes aphids congregating at the tender growing tips and any powdery mildew that has established itself on these same tips. These pruned tips should be removed from the garden and burned or put into the garbage.

Maintaining the size and productivity of the plant is a two-step process. Each winter, prune out two older, less productive branches and all but the strongest two new shoots. Then, cut back the leaders by about one-half to a bud that faces out (away from the center of the plant) and shorten the laterals. If these simple steps are followed, the plant will have six to eight strong, young shoots that should produce ample amounts of berries or currants.

I suspect that many gardeners have never properly pruned their bushes to begin with. Most beginners simply plant the little fellows directly from the nursery and watch them grow up. With red and white cur-

*Keep strawberry beds weed-free and the plants will reward your efforts many-fold.*

## GOOSEBERRY RENOVATION

 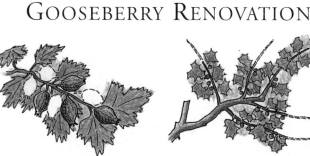  

| | | | |
|---|---|---|---|
| *In the spring of the first year, cut back all leaders by half.* | *In the summer, fruits can be thinned to increase their size.* | *In the summer, fruiting laterals can be cut back to 5 or 6 leaves to open plant and control aphids.* | *In the second and subsequent springs, cut back all leaders by half.* |

rants as well as gooseberries, a plant will yield fruit without pruning of any kind, but if the bush grows wild and rampant, the yields will decline. Pruning will increase yields, keep the bush healthier and make harvesting much easier.

# STRAWBERRIES

STRAWBERRIES ARE THE WEEDIEST CROP IN the garden, but pulling the weeds has its rewards—there are few things as satisfying on a hot summer's day as picking a juicy berry from the center of the fruit-set and letting it melt in your mouth.

The key to growing strawberries is to keep the plants weed-free. Mulching the beds or pulling weeds are the two most practical options for the home gardener, but even these can be difficult if weeds take root among the plants. However, even if weeds get established, it is not too difficult to clean them out, and it is certainly less work to weed routinely than to renovate an entire bed.

If a bed has become overgrown, you have a couple of options: either buy or propagate new plants and prepare a bed in another site or renovate the existing bed. Renovation, although simpler, is not always worthwhile, because strawberry plants are productive for only a few years and because the soil often becomes infected with viruses and bacteria. While disease problems are more serious for commercial growers, home gardeners will still find it prudent to move their strawberry bed every three to four years.

If you choose the first option—buying or propagating plants—you will want to prepare the soil thoroughly by fertilizing and tilling or by double-digging. Set plants 18 inches apart in rows spaced every 3 feet. Make sure the crown of the plant is not covered with soil, as it may rot and the plant will die. Water the new plants well and remove any flowers the first year. Picking off the flowers will prevent fruit formation, but it will encourage the development of roots and runners. Subsequent harvests will be more bountiful. A normal harvest is 8 to 10 ounces of fruit per plant. Runners are formed in July after fruiting is finished, and these runners can be used to propagate your own plants.

If your strawberry patch is a mass of weeds and tangled plants that is not worth salvaging, consider preparing a new bed and propagating plants to fill it. Propagating strawberries is not difficult and can be done in one of two ways. In the first approach, merely look for the young developing plants on the runners as they begin to root. Carefully sever these plantlets from the mother plant and move them into your freshly prepared soil. These newly moved and hesitantly rooted plants will need daily watering and protection from the scorching sun. One way to shade them is to cut open a white plastic garbage bag (the size for a kitchen trash can) and drape it over a plant, or plants, like a bonnet. Pin down the corners of the bag with small stakes. Despite your best efforts, some of your transplants may not survive, so set out a few extras to replace any plants that fail.

In the second method, you do not cut the plantlets from the mother plant until they are well rooted. Success rates are higher with this approach, but the job is more involved. First, fill some small flowerpots with potting soil and sink them to the rim in the ground around a mother plant. Then, train the runners thrown by the plant to stay in the flowerpots. A twig or a bent paper clip looped over the runner and pushed into the soil will hold the runner in place. (Roots will form from the runners.) Check the pots every day to make sure the soil does not dry out. Once the runners are well rooted, cut them away from the mother plant. Give them a few more weeks to grow, then transplant them (usually they are ready around the middle of August). They should quickly establish themselves in the newly prepared bed.

If you want to renovate your plants without moving the entire strawberry patch, the following system will work quite well. Immediately after the harvest, divide the bed lengthwise into two sections or rows. Remove the plants and weeds and thoroughly renovate the soil in one section. (See Chapter Ten, page 120, for details on soil renovation.) Then, as runners develop from the remaining plants, train them into

# STRAWBERRY RENOVATION

*Immediately after harvest, divide the bed in half and remove the plants and weeds from one section.*
*As runners from the remaining plants develop, train them into the renovated section, Bed A.*

*In the second year, remove the older plants, renovate their half of the bed and train*
*the runners from the younger plants into this newly prepared section, Bed B.*

the newly renovated section using twigs or paper clips. When the plantlets root, cut them away from the mother plants. The next year, after you harvest berries from the mother plants, remove these older plants and renovate the soil.

Meanwhile, the plantlets that you established the year before (in Bed A in the illustration) will begin to send out runners. As these grow, train them into the newly renovated ground (Bed B). Both sections of the patch will then be renovated and filled with young, productive plants.

Dividing a bed into three sections and renovating one section a year is an even better, although more complicated, approach. It will allow plants to bear for two years before being replaced. This ongoing renewal process will help control weeds and will continue to develop a supply of young plants. The end result—more and better strawberries—will be ample reward.

CHAPTER NINE

# AWNS

*"I believe a leaf of grass is no less than
the journey-work of the stars"*

W. WHITMAN (1819-1892),
***Song of the Open Road***

GRASS IS SUCH A DURABLE, ALL-PURPOSE GROUND cover that we often take it for granted. We tread on it with soccer shoes and football spikes, we clobber it with golf clubs, and we expect it to endure, as if its leaves were made of wire instead of chlorophyll. Yet when we want to stretch out on a lawn and contemplate the clouds, we expect the softness of a feather bed.

Grass is expected to be both tender and tough. But it has specific cultural needs that cannot be ignored. If we take it for granted, we will soon find out there is nothing under the grass but hard ground. No amount of fertilizer or chemicals will restore a lawn if it has been improperly watered or mowed. The basic cultural requirements of grass are simple enough to address once they are understood and appreciated.

From a caretaking or renovation point of view, lawns might be divided into three categories: high, medium and low maintenance. Each will satisfy a different expectation for a lawn and each requires a different

*We often take grass for granted, yet it has cultural needs that should not be ignored.*

investment in labor and, to some extent, a specific variety of grass.

High-maintenance lawns epitomize the grounds of elegant estates or the homes of compulsive landscapers. The grass must be heavily fertilized and frequently watered—commonly with an automatic, in-ground irrigation system. It must be sprayed with chemicals to kill insects and diseases and mowed at least twice a week to maintain a grass height of about 1 inch. In areas north of USDA zone 7, high-maintenance lawns are often planted primarily with Kentucky bluegrass (and some red fescue), a variety that depends on coddling to thrive.

With a medium-maintenance lawn, the objective is to keep the grass green and healthy but not to create a completely weed- and insect-free environment. The grass is allowed to grow taller than in a high-maintenance setting. Mowing is a weekly or every 10-day chore, so the grass has an average height of roughly 2 inches. Fertilizer is applied two or three times a year, rather than the six or eight times required for a high-maintenance look. Chemicals to discourage weeds and insects are put on about once a year or whenever an application is recommended by a lawn care company. For northern lawns, a blend of one or more fescue types with some bluegrass and, perhaps, some perennial rye is frequently planted. Medium-maintenance lawns are the most common lawns in the landscape of suburban North America.

Low-maintenance lawns, meanwhile, are rarely the jewel of any neighborhood. By definition, they receive little attention. They are green in the spring and fall if rains are adequate, but they are allowed to go brown during summer droughts. Because growth is not encouraged, the grass may be mowed only six to eight times a year, depending on rainfall. Fertilizer might be applied once in the spring, but pesticides and herbicides are not part of the regimen nor is irrigation. You don't water a lawn if you don't particularly want it to grow. Depending on the region, perennial ryegrass

and red fescue, which is tolerant of some drought and soil acidity, may be common in the low-maintenance lawn. These grasses are often joined by whatever other greenery happens to take root.

Having defined these three maintenance categories, you might say that most lawns do not fall neatly into any one of them. Your approach may be some combination of the three. Nevertheless, it may be useful to keep these scenarios in mind so that you can picture the amount of work required to revive a tired lawn and maintain it at a certain standard.

# GRASS VARIETIES

THE GRASS SEED BUSINESS IN NORTH AMERICA is huge. In the Willamette Valley of Oregon alone, thousands of acres of cropland are allocated to growing grass for its seed. Seed companies invest millions of dollars researching new varieties that are more drought-tolerant, disease-resistant, finer-bladed and even shorter, to reduce the chore of mowing.

In the last 10 years, many new grass varieties have been introduced that are bred for the climatological requirements of a particular region. The challenge in the South has been to find varieties that can tolerate the heat and humidity of the summer. For northern lawns, breeders have sought varieties that will withstand the cold yet flourish in the summer.

In years past, most lawns in the North were planted with some blend of Kentucky bluegrass and red fescue. Bluegrass remains popular for high-maintenance lawns. Red fescue, both what is called chewing red fescue and creeping red fescue, is still commonly planted. However, breeders are working with other types of fescues, including tall fescue, which is very drought-tolerant, and hard fescue, which is shade-tolerant. Breeders have also introduced a number of new strains of perennial ryegrass.

For parts of the Midwest and Great Plains and

## Common Lawn Grasses

| | Kentucky Bluegrass | Red Fescue | Perennial Ryegrass |
|---|---|---|---|
| **Mowing Height** | 1½" to 2" | 2" to 3" | 2" to 3" |
| **Nitrogen Requirement per 1,000 sq.ft.** | 1-2 lbs. | 1 lb. | 1 lb. |
| **Soil Moisture** | Requires good drainage; does not like drought | Tolerates moisture but not wet, poorly drained soils; tolerates drought | Tolerates moisture but prefers good drainage; tolerates drought |
| **Light** | Full sun | Tolerates some shade | Full sun to light shade |
| **Wear Tolerance** | Good | Medium | Excellent |
| **Acidic Soil Tolerance** | No tolerance for acidic soils | Tolerates a pH as low as 5.5 | Tolerates a pH as low as 5.3 |
| **Disease Tolerance** | Good | Good | Good |
| **Winter Hardiness** | Excellent | Excellent | Excellent |

other arid areas, researchers are working with a number of strains of buffalo grass. Buffalo grass is native to North America, unlike most other common species of lawn grass, which originated in Europe, and is extremely drought-resistant. Breeders are trying to preserve that quality while developing strains that are more fine-bladed, darker green and more tolerant of being closely mowed. In the South, research has focused on new strains of Bermuda grass, Saint Augustine grass and other species suitable for intense summer heat.

Climate is a primary consideration when choosing grass seed, and garden centers are not likely to stock seed that is inappropriate for their region. But beyond climate, it is important to take into account the exposure of the lawn—whether it will have full sun or partial shade, whether the site is damp or well drained and the type and amount of use or abuse the grass will have to endure. Also keep in mind that some grass types need more coddling than others. Planting a blend of varieties will produce a lawn with more insect and disease resistance than a pure stand of one variety.

In northern areas, perennial ryegrass has become an important component (as much as 20 percent) of seed mixes for sunny lawns that must withstand a lot of foot traffic or rough play. Perennial ryegrass germinates very quickly and helps hold topsoil in place while more slowly germinating species get established. For shady, wet areas, mixes often include a small percentage of turf timothy and rough-stalked meadow grass, also called rough-stalked bluegrass, neither of which need to be closely trimmed but can be left on the rough and tall side.

## Cultural Needs

Grass needs a certain amount of care, but ironically, probably more lawns decline from too much attention than from neglect. Across much of North America, lawns are being loved to death. They are being overfertilized, overwatered and repeatedly mown at a crew-cut height. Problems from this overzealous approach may not be immediately appar-

*Lawns that are regularly irrigated will be lush and deeply rooted.*

ent. In fact, the grass may look lush and grow quickly for a few years. Only after several seasons of overfeeding and repeated shearing will it begin to weaken and allow weeds and disease to become established.

For the health of the grass, water a lawn only when it begins to show signs of drought. (These signs include a darkening green color and a curling of the grass leaf.) When you do water your lawn, give the grass a thorough soaking to encourage deep, thick roots. Repeated shallow watering encourages shallow roots, which leaves the grass more susceptible to drought than if it were left to fend for itself.

Irrigate at the rate of 1 inch of water per week, and deliver that water slowly, either in two equal applications or one long soaking so the water will not run off before it can be absorbed by the soil. To deliver an appropriate amount of water, measure the output from

your lawn sprinkler: set a flat-bottomed container under the spray of your sprinkler and time how long it takes to fill the container with an inch of water. Time your irrigation accordingly.

Giving a lawn adequate nutrition is not much more complicated than providing enough water. Using any fertilizer of approximately a 4-1-2 ratio, apply enough fertilizer so that every 1,000 square feet of lawn is nourished with 2 pounds of nitrogen a year. Apply this amount in three installments. To meet the needs of the average lawn, apply ½ pound in April or May, ½ pound in late July and 1 pound in early November.

A third important part of lawn care involves minimizing the buildup of thatch. Thatch is an accumulation of dead leaves, stems and grass roots just above the soil line. Too much of this old organic matter will cause grass roots to grow out of the soil and become established in the thatch. This will make the roots more vulnerable to drought and more likely to be injured by mowing and foot traffic.

Poor drainage or cutting off too much grass in one mowing are the usual causes of thatch. Soggy conditions discourage worms and soil bacteria from breaking down the organic matter. Any other conditions that reduce the worm population, such as soil compaction or excess lawn chemicals, can also lead to thatch.

Thatch can be removed with a vigorous raking. A more permanent solution, however, involves addressing the causes of the problem. If thatch is due to a heavy clay soil holding excess moisture, you may have to dig up the lawn and install drainage tiles. Ideally, the answer will be simpler, and you might only need to reduce the amount of irrigation.

Of all the lawn maintenance chores, the most common is mowing. While the mechanics of this job are well understood, people are surprisingly ignorant of its impact on grass. Improper mowing can leave grass susceptible to drought, insects and disease.

Keeping grass short tends to make the turf thicker, since pruning stimulates new growth. However, a short cut also means shallower plant roots because there is less leaf area to gather sunlight and produce growth energy. The plants will have fewer reserves to endure drought or a harsh winter. At the same time, grass that is cut too short and heavily watered will be very lush. This tender growth is a dinner invitation to pests and disease.

As a general rule, keep grass at a height of about 2 inches during the heat of the summer. This may seem a bit taller than usual, but the longer blades will mean deeper roots, which will give the plants more drought tolerance. Longer blades will also shade the roots and thus reduce moisture loss. In the spring and fall, you can keep the grass shorter—at about 1½ inches.

Mowing ought to be part of a regular routine rather than a major job once every three or four weeks. Giving the grass a dramatic haircut will shock it and also

create an excess of organic matter, leading to a possible buildup of thatch. If you come back from vacation to find an overgrown lawn, trim it gradually with two or three cuttings spaced a day or two apart, rather than mowing it all down in a single pass. Rarely is it advisable to cut a lawn by more than one-third of its length in any one mowing.

A dull lawn mower is another invitation to trouble, because it rips the grass instead of cutting it cleanly. Ripped leaves are susceptible to disease organisms. Keeping the mower blade sharp is part of the prescription for a healthy lawn.

If you are following a medium- or low-maintenance approach, leave clippings on the lawn. They contain many nutrients that will benefit the soil and reduce fertilizer needs by 20 to 35 percent. The clippings also attract earthworms. The more worms, the more the soil is enriched by their waste, or castings, and the more quickly they can break down thatch. There can, of course, be too much of a good thing. If more than ½ inch of clippings remains after each mowing, they may mat and smother the grass. Try cutting your lawn more often or reducing the level of irrigation and fertilizer.

In the spring, many gardeners feel a compulsion to rush out and work on their lawns as soon as the snow melts or the rain stops. Resist the urge. Give the ground time to dry. Running a roller or mower across the lawn and even walking on it too early can compact the soil and damage the plants' roots.

Once the lawn is firm, rake away winter debris. Then wait until the grass is 2½ to 3 inches high before mowing. This allows the leaves time to grow and produce energy that can feed the roots and help them recover from the ravages of winter.

As the season progresses, a shady lawn should be kept about ½ inch taller than a lawn in full sun. Shade reduces the energy grass can produce, so the plants need more leaf area to compensate for the loss of sunlight.

# PEST CONTROLS

## CHINCH BUGS

Lawns are troubled by only a few serious pests, and for the most part, they can be easily discouraged. The most common threat to weakened lawns is the chinch bug, which sucks sap from grass blades and can cause plants to wither and die. Chinch bug nymphs hatch and begin feeding in May, but their damage does not become widespread or evident until later in the summer when, as temperatures rise, the growth of new grass leaves slows down. When they hatch, the bugs are about ¼ inch long and reddish. They mature to black, with a white spot on the back between the wings. They are difficult to detect because they dive for cover into the thatch layer when disturbed.

A good way to find out whether or not you have chinch bugs is to cut the ends off a large metal can and sink the can into the ground so its top rim is about an inch above the grass. Flood the can with water; any chinch bugs in the lawn will float to the surface. Another way is to flood a suspected chinch bug injury site and place a white cloth over the site. The chinch bugs will climb up onto the cloth, where they can be easily identified.

Where chinch bugs are active, the grass will yellow and die. Injury sites appear as sunken patches, usually beginning in July, and may seem to be spreading from flower gardens, hedgerows or trees. Close inspection of grass blades in the outer rings of each patch will show damage on individual blades. Take immediate action or by August the chinch bug population will be very strong and the lawn will be heavily scarred.

Chinch bugs can be controlled in several different ways. The first is to flood the lawn—the entire lawn, if it is small, or section by section if it is too large to completely soak all at once. Flooding will bring the bugs to the top of the grass where they can be sprayed with an insecticidal soap. You may have to spray several times because the soap has no residual effect. Read the label and follow the directions carefully. (See Chapter Eleven, page 133, for more information on insecticidal soaps.)

A second strategy involves flooding the lawn, then applying a chemical registered for the control of chinch bugs. Diazinon and chlorpyrifos have been approved in some areas for use on chinch bugs, but it is a good idea to check with a local garden center and read the label before spraying. There is no point in using a chemical that does not control the problem.

The third approach is long term and systemic, involving cultural practices, not chemicals. Chinch bugs favor lush, succulent grass—lawns that have been over-fertilized and overirrigated. If you reduce the water and the fertilizer, you will reduce the chinch bug problem.

## GRUBS

Three types of grubs are of greatest concern for grass: June beetle larvae, Japanese beetle larvae and European chafer larvae. The June beetle larva is a C-shaped grub with a brown head and three pairs of long legs. It takes three years for this larva to develop into an adult, and all this time it is feeding under the sod of the lawn. The adult June beetle, which feeds on the foliage of trees and shrubs, is about 1 inch long, dark brown and attracted to lights at night—this is the bug that buzzes and thwacks against the screen door in summer.

Japanese beetle larvae are similar to those of June beetles, but the mature beetle is only about half the size of the adult June beetle. The Japanese beetle larva takes only one year to mature. The bronze-green adult emerges from the soil in July to feed on the foliage of numerous fruiting plants and ornamentals.

Larvae of the European chafer also resemble larvae of the June beetle, but they are only about half the size. The adult, too, resembles a small June beetle. It does not feed on trees and shrubs, but it can be found swarming with June beetles in late June and early July.

Suspect damage from grubs (it doesn't matter which kind) if irregular patches of lawn gradually turn brown in the summer. The discoloration is caused by grubs feeding on the roots of the grass. If the lawn is dug up in shallow patches, it probably means that skunks have been scratching around for their supper. While skunks will consume some grubs, they may not be the ideal solution to this problem. More complete control can be obtained with predatory nematodes. (A description of these tiny creatures and their contributions to the health of lawns and gardens can be found in Chapter Eleven, page 134.)

Japanese beetle grubs can be discouraged by dusting the lawn with a powder carrying a strain of *Bacillus* bacteria. Sold under various names, such as Doom, the bacteria introduce milky disease to the grubs. Apply the powder in a grid pattern, sifting it onto the grass in spots about 3 feet apart. Milky disease spreads most quickly in warm soil (above 70 degrees F) with a near-neutral (7.0) pH. Where soils are acidic or relatively cool, apply the powder at a heavier than recommended rate. The spores perpetuate themselves and can live in the soil indefinitely, but it may take several years before they multiply enough to eliminate most of the grubs.

If you choose a chemical option for grub control, apply the product sometime between late June and early July, just as the beetles are laying their eggs. A good raking to remove any thatch and a thorough watering will prepare the turf for treatment. After spraying, water the soil again to wash the chemicals down to the level of the grubs and eggs. Before applying any chemicals, read the label to familiarize yourself with recommended techniques and precautions. General advice can be obtained from local extension service personnel, master gardeners or garden centers.

If grub damage is detected during hot, dry weather, irrigate and fertilize the lawn to maintain its vigor and help the grass resist degradation.

# DISEASE CONTROLS

THERE ARE MANY TURF DISEASES THAT CAN strike the intensively managed golf green, but a medium-maintenance lawn is seldom attacked if cared for properly. Growing thick, healthy, deep-rooted grass gives the plants more strength to fight off diseases.

Of all the lawn ailments a gardener is likely to face, a fungus called fairy ring may be the most troublesome. It grows on decaying organic matter and starts in one small spot of the lawn with a white fungal growth, often in the shape of a ring. It gradually expands at a rate of 12 to 18 inches a year, retaining a circular shape. This can be a tough fungus to eliminate because there are few chemical options. Heavy raking, aerating and frequent watering can retard its spread. Fertilizing the area and reseeding helps to stimulate the growth of new grass and, in turn, repair some of the damage. The only total solution is to remove the grass and soil to a depth of 12 to 18 inches, replace it with fungus-free loam and reseed.

Fairy ring is sometimes confused with a disease called snow mold. Both appear in circular patches, but snow mold is evident in the spring, after the snow has melted, as white-gray mold patches. A vigorous raking and topdressing of seed will totally eliminate this temporary problem. Do not use chemical controls. Moderate irrigation and fertilizer applications, especially late in the summer, will reduce the incidence of snow mold. Raking away thatch and mowing in the fall until all leaf growth stops will also help.

Dollar spot is another fungus that spreads in a circular pattern. While it is not common on home lawns, it is sometimes evident during hot, humid weather. The most apparent symptom is cobweb-like growths seen early in the morning, before the dew dries. Grass low in nitrogen is most prone to this fungus. The cure is to feed the lawn a water-soluble fertilizer that can be quickly absorbed.

While there are other fungi that spread in a circular pattern, the most common problem is perpetrated not by fungus but by Fido. What might be politely termed "dog injury" shows up as a yellow circle of dead grass with an outer ring of lush growth. Ureal nitrogen in a heavy concentration burns the grass at the center of the circle but stimulates growth at the outer edge, where the concentration is diluted. Most damage can be repaired in several weeks with regular watering, then light fertilizing. In extreme cases, you may need to topdress and reseed the area in the manner described below ("Renovating Your Lawn"). A long-term cure can be achieved only by keeping dogs off the lawn.

Moss in grass is a symptom of heavy shade, low fertility or acidic, damp or poorly drained soil. Lime can be applied to reduce the soil acidity. Fertilizer will improve fertility. But if shade or poor drainage is the problem, there may be few options to improve the situation short of cutting down trees or digging up the yard and installing perforated pipe, also called drainage tile, to move groundwater away from the area. Instead of struggling to change basic conditions, try growing plants that thrive in the existing environment.

# RENOVATING YOUR LAWN

TREATING YOUR LAWN EACH SPRING TO A topdressing of grass seed and organic matter will produce turf that rarely, if ever, needs extensive renovation. This preventative care is easily administered. For every 1,000 square feet of lawn, mix 4 to 6 cubic feet of peat moss with 2 pounds of grass seed and the appropriate amount of granulated fertilizer. To this basic mix, add 2 to 4 cubic feet of vermiculite or sharp sand. The sand is excellent for improving the surface drainage in clay soils. You can also add compost—as much as you can spare—up to one-quarter of the volume of the peat. Instead of using compost, you can buy

*To produce excellent turf, treat your lawn each spring to a topdressing of grass seed and organic matter.*

bags of composted manure. Add two 20-pound bags for every 6 cubic feet of peat moss. Mix these ingredients together thoroughly in a wheelbarrow or on a tarp and spread them thinly on the lawn (to a depth of about ½ inch). Use a lawn rake to incorporate the mix or go over it with rotary mower set to a height of 2½ inches to scatter the mix around. Once the mix is spread, keep the lawn lightly watered to help the grass get established.

Lawns that have been ignored for years or that are heavily used may need to be renovated from time to time. How much work is involved depends on the condition of the grass, the reasons for its deterioration and the expectations of the homeowner.

If the grass is basically in good shape with, perhaps, some damage from chinch bugs, it can be returned to uniform vigor with a small amount of renovation. If chinch bugs have attacked some areas, deal with them in the summer, as explained on page 114. Then, in the spring, start a renovation program. First, after raking away any dense thatch, begin to increase the number of times you apply fertilizer. Increasing the number of applications does not mean putting on more fertilizer; it means splitting the recommended amount into five or six applications, instead of one or two.

Increasing the amount of water you put on the lawn should also stimulate renewal growth. Once the turf has regained its vigor, cut the watering regimen back to a normal level of about 1 inch per week.

When a lawn is somewhat worn, neglected or scarred with a number of bare patches, a more thorough renovation is required. This is a simple two-step process that is best undertaken in the spring or late summer in areas north of zone 6 or in the early fall in areas south of zone 5.

First, rake over the areas where the grass has died to remove all the thatch and loosen the soil. Then

sprinkle grass seed at a rate of 3 to 5 pounds per 1,000 square feet, or 1 ounce per square yard. A hand-operated seeder, which casts the seed as you turn the handle, is useful for seeding large areas. Walking the area in one direction, then going in a perpendicular direction, helps distribute the seed evenly. After seeding, lightly rake the area to mix in the seed. Sprinkle on a thin topdressing of soil (no deeper than ¼ inch). Then, if possible, use a light roller to smooth and compact the surface to help the seed stay in place and improve contact with the soil. Water the area with a fine mist spray and try to keep the soil from drying out until the new grass is established.

Before any renovation can succeed, the underlying causes of poor grass growth need to be addressed. One of the first steps in determining basic growth problems is to conduct a soil test. Take small soil samples from several places in the lawn and combine them in a clean container. Submit the sample to a cooperative extension service lab or a local garden club for a pH test. Such tests are often free or inexpensive and will provide an indication of whether lime is needed to change the pH to a more favorable level. (A neutral pH is measured as 7.0. Progressively lower numbers indicate increasingly acidic conditions; readings above 7.0 indicate alkaline conditions. Grass thrives in soil with a pH range from about 5.5 to 7.0, depending on the variety.)

Applications of dolomitic lime can "sweeten" the soil, or make it more alkaline. If poor drainage is the problem, you might need to lighten the soil with sand or compost. Or, in extreme cases, you may be faced with the prospect of putting in drainage tiles.

When assessing your lawn conditions, keep in mind that not every setting can be made suitable for grass. So why spend considerable time and money in a losing effort? Lawns, after all, are not the only option. A poorly drained site might be turned into a shimmering little pond. An area of acidic soils near a stand of conifers might be planted with blueberries, rhododen-

*In spring and fall, keep grass mowed to a height of about 1½ inches. In the summer, allow the blades to grow a bit taller.*

drons or azaleas, which happily grow in ground with a low pH. In other settings, flowers, shrubs or evergreens might be more appropriate than grass. Use your imagination. Try to get beyond the stereotype of a front lawn as shown on a box of grass seed.

If weeds are the culprit, you have a few restoration options. You can eliminate all the greenery—weeds and grass—with herbicides. Though not a favorite remedy for many gardeners, some herbicides are relatively benign to the environment, such as the compound glyphosate, which is found in widely marketed herbicides like Roundup. (See Chapter Eleven, page

130, for a further discussion of weed-control options.)

There are also nonchemical options for eliminating greenery. One is to simply cover the lawn with clear plastic for the entire summer. Enough heat will build up under the plastic to pasteurize the soil and kill most plant roots and many seeds. We have used this technique in our nursery to sterilize soil beds, and the beds have remained weed-free for several years. The plastic sheeting is earthworm-friendly, so worms can leave the area to avoid the heat but will return once the plastic is removed and the ground is replanted.

A third approach to total renovation is to remove the sod. This involves a great deal of work, although the results can be preferable to either of the other options because you can begin anew on bare ground. Sod-cutting machines are available from some equipment rental centers and speed the removal along.

While you are getting rid of the weeds, begin considering how you will reestablish a carpet of grass. Will you plant seed or put down sod? Sod is established turf, grown in pampered conditions, then cut out of the nursery field, rolled up and delivered to your door. It is sold by the square foot and is several times more expensive than planting seed. However, sod creates an almost instant lawn.

If you decide to use sod, prepare your soil with a 5-20-20 fertilizer applied at the rate of 25 pounds per 1,000 square feet. Lightly water this in, and be ready to work when the sod delivery truck arrives. Sod should be put in place immediately or its tender roots will quickly die. Lay the sections tightly but do not try to stretch the sod. It will shrink when it dries and there will be gaps between pieces if they have been stretched.

After laying the sod, go over it with a roller. This is critical to achieving good contact between the sod roots and the soil. Then thoroughly soak the sod immediately after you put it down and repeat this watering daily for 10 to 14 days, depending on the temperature, sunshine and quality and depth of the soil under the sod. If laid in the spring or fall, sod will require much less water and be more likely to take hold than if laid in the heat of summer. Do not walk on the sod for at least two weeks to avoid damaging the newly emerging roots, but once established, treat and tend sod like any other turf.

If you decide to seed your lawn, try to schedule the job for late summer or early fall in climates north of zone 6. In warmer areas, the job can be undertaken later in the fall or in early winter. Conditions of cool air temperatures and warm soil stimulate fast germination and healthy root growth. Early spring is the second best time to plant a lawn.

In addition to temperature, soil bed preparation is a key to good germination. Follow the same fertilizer recommendations for sod (25 pounds of 5-20-20 per 1,000 square feet), then lightly roll the soil to make a firm bed on which to broadcast the seed. Apply the seed, either by hand or with a mechanical seeder, at the rate of 3 to 5 pounds per 1,000 square feet. Then roll the soil again. This will not only improve contact between the seed and the soil, but it will also compress the top ¼ inch or so of soil to give it more density and make it slower to dry out.

When the new grass is 3 inches tall, apply fertilizer with a 10-2-6 ratio at the rate of 5 pounds per 1,000 square feet, then mow the grass to a height of 2 inches. If the seeding was done in the fall, do not mow the grass until spring unless it puts on a spurt of growth and reaches 3 or 4 inches. In May or June, trim it to about 2 inches. Do not use any herbicides for at least six to eight weeks after seeding.

Lawns can become a compulsion for many home-owners. At the sight of a dandelion—even in someone else's yard—they reach for a weeder or a can of herbicide. They spray and mow and water and manicure until you wonder why they don't just put down artificial turf and be done with it. I recommend a more laissez-faire attitude. Why get neurotic about grass? Do your best, but if that's not good enough, remember that the sun will still come up in the morning.

# CHAPTER TEN

# SOIL RENOVATION

*"I would rather be tied to the soil as
another man's serf, even a poor man's, who
hadn't much to live on himself, than be King
of all these, the dead and destroyed."*

HOMER (NINTH CENTURY B.C.)
*Odyssey*

SOIL IS GOOD STUFF—THE ELEMENTAL FOOD, THE foundation of every garden. Yet apart from the praise lavished on it by such writers as Homer, soil has been a much undervalued commodity. To the true gardener, nothing is quite so dear as freshly dug soil on a clear spring day. Even if your appreciation is less enthusiastic, you sooner or later have to acknowledge that the success of your horticultural endeavors depends on good soil. What follows is a basic course on making old soil new again.

To understand how and why garden soil needs renovation, it is necessary to understand soil texture. There are three sizes of soil particles. Clay, the smallest (less than .00008 inches in diameter) combines with silt (between and .00008 and .002 inches in diameter) and sand (between .002 and .08 inches in diameter) to form soil. These individual particles

*To a true gardener, nothing is quite so dear as freshly dug soil.*

form aggregates or granules. If the majority of combined granules are clay, the soil is referred to as a clay soil. If the majority are sand or silt, the soil is referred to as a sandy or a silt soil. To understand the dynamics of these granules, imagine a soil composed of only sand. The large particles would fit loosely together, with a lot of air between them—like dozens of basketballs in a huge container. Because of the large air spaces, water can move through a sandy soil quickly. The spaces also provide plenty of room for plant roots. These are good characteristics of sandy soils. However, because they drain so quickly, sandy soils must be watered frequently.

At the opposite end of the size spectrum are clay soils. Compared to a container of basketballs, clay soils are like a container of golf balls, with all the particles fitting closely together. Clay soil does not drain well because water tends to remain in the tight spaces between the particles. Once the water does drain out, it is difficult for more water to filter in. The soil becomes hard and impermeable. Roots have to fight to get into the small air spaces in search of nutrients, and they risk being drowned or parched.

Silt soils are somewhere between the two extremes of sand and clay. Water moves through silt more slowly than through sand but faster than through clay. Silt soils compact less readily than clay. A good garden loam should be composed of all three constituents. Ideally, it should be approximately 15 percent clay, 40 percent sand and 40 percent silt and have about 5 percent organic content.

Analyzing the soil in your garden is the first step in deciding whether modifications are necessary and, if so, where to begin. Here is one way to make an analysis: From several different parts of your garden, take a small trowel full of soil and thoroughly mix these samples in a pail. Fill a large glass jar, such as a coffee container, one-third to one-half full with this sample mixture, and top the jar off with water. Cover the jar and shake the mix thoroughly to suspend all the soil particles in the water. Then, put the jar aside and let the particles settle.

Sand is the heaviest particle and will settle first. Within several hours you will be able to see a distinct layer of sand underneath the silt, which will settle on top of the sand layer. Clay, the smallest of the particles, will take several days to settle. (Organic matter will either remain floating or will eventually rest on top of the clay.) When all the materials have settled, you will be able to determine the composition of your soil and estimate what percentage of each material it contains.

# IMPROVING SOIL STRUCTURE

WITH TIME, EVEN GOOD GARDEN SOILS CAN become compacted. Walking on the soil, working it when it is wet, running equipment across it and even watering can compress soil particles. This leaves the soil with less air and fewer spaces for plant roots and makes the soil less able to absorb water.

The single best way to correct compaction and improve the structure of any garden soil is by double-digging and, if necessary, by adding various amendments, such as sand, compost or gypsum, during the digging process.

For example, clay soil can be improved by gradually adding small quantities of sand. Masonry sand or regular fill sand works well. Spread a ⅛-inch layer over an entire bed or section of the garden and work it into the soil. Substantially changing the composition of the soil is a long-term process. Adding too much sand at any one time will result in pockets of sand and pockets of clay—a condition worse than pure clay. Add small amounts of sand whenever you turn over your beds until the desired soil structure is achieved. Incorporating gypsum at the rate of 8 ounces to 1 square yard of soil will also help break up clay soil.

Working organic matter into the garden is another

*A weekly feeding of manure tea, applied from a watering can, will benefit any heavily flowering plants.*

method of breaking down clay and of improving the structure and water-holding capacity of very sandy soil. Organic matter continues to decompose, however, so it must be frequently replaced. In fact, continually adding composted materials is a wonderful way to maintain the structure and fertility of any soil.

In our gardens, I add one shovelful of compost (a mixture of chicken manure, kitchen scraps, peat moss and wood shavings) for every three shovelfuls of soil that I dig. I used to add it as I was shoveling, but now I know how much I need for each bed and I simply spread it over the bed before I begin to dig.

I double-dig our kitchen garden beds every two

years but turn them over one spit deep every spring. (A "spit" equals the depth of a shovel blade.) The perennial borders are dug before they are planted and are redug in spots when plants have to be moved or divided. I completely double-dig a perennial flower bed only during a total renovation.

## DOUBLE-DIGGING

Double-digging essentially means loosening the soil to a depth of two shovel blades, or about 12 to 18 inches, depending on the shovel. Initially, double-digging heavy or compacted soil can be quite laborious.

# DOUBLE-DIGGING TECHNIQUE

*Loosening the soil to a depth of two shovel blades can make a dramatic improvement in the quality of your plants.*

*Excavate a trench about one foot wide and about two shovel blades deep across the end of the bed and leave the soil beside the bed or put it in a wheelbarrow.*

*Dig a second trench of the same dimensions as the first, and use the excavated soil from the second to fill in the first trench.*

*Continue trenching the length of the bed. Add soil amendments as you go. Collect any rocks and weeds in a bucket.*

*Use the soil from the first trench to fill in the last one, then rake the bed smooth.*

But once an area has been double-dug, subsequent digging is much easier. Double-digging is most commonly done in gardens that are arranged in beds rather than open rows, but the approach may be used in any garden.

The first step in double-digging is to excavate a trench about 1 foot wide and about two shovel blades deep across the end of a bed (see illustration on facing page, Step One). Leave the excavated soil beside the bed for later use (or, if the bed is large, move the soil to the other end with a wheelbarrow). Then dig another trench of the same width and depth right next to the first one. Use the soil from the second trench to fill in the first one (Step Two). Keep working down the bed, trench by trench. Remove any rocks and weed roots as you go, and put the weeds in a wheelbarrow or bucket so they will not be forgotten and take root again (Step Three). To increase organic matter, add compost, manure or peat moss as you fill in each trench. Add sand to lighten a clay soil. After excavating the last trench, fill it with the soil taken from the first one. Then, rake the bed so it is smooth and level (Step Four), and the job is finished. The soil level will be higher after digging, but it will settle as weather and cultivation take their toll.

If, for any reason, you doubt the value of double-digging, I suggest you try it first on at least one bed. You'll note a dramatic improvement in the size and quality of your plants.

# SOIL FERTILITY

GETTING THE FERTILITY OF YOUR SOIL TESTED is a useful first step in any garden renovation project. For less than $20, many cooperative extension service laboratories will analyze a soil sample for pH, major and many minor nutrients, and organic matter. The results enable you to choose plants suitable for your soil and to talk more knowledgeably with pro-

fessional nurserymen about adjusting the soil conditions for the plants you already have.

The accuracy and detail of a lab analysis cannot be duplicated with one of the small testing kits found at garden centers. These units, which require that you mix soil and a reagent in a test tube, are notoriously unreliable. They depend on an unscientific comparison of colored liquid in the test tube with blocks of color on a chart, which you hope hasn't faded in the sun.

If you choose not to send a soil sample off for analysis, you can simply assume your plants need compost and a bit of bone meal and blood meal and provide them with a routine feeding. Good nutrition will promote better foliage colors and bigger flowers and, most importantly, it will give plants more resilience against insects and disease. Our rule of thumb is to cover the garden with ¼ inch of compost every spring.

We also feed individual plants according to the following general formula: Every spring, small perennials get a small handful of bone and blood meal and larger or older plants get two handfuls; small shrubs get two handfuls of bone and blood meal and larger shrubs get three or four handfuls. The bigger the plant, the more food it needs. With bone meal and blood meal, it is very hard to overfeed a plant and burn it. Simply toss the food around the base of the plant, brush most of the powder off the foliage (it doesn't seem to hurt the plant, it just looks terrible) and relax knowing that the garden is going to grow more vigorously.

If my plants need a quick pick-me-up in the middle of the summer, I use a manure tea or liquid fish fertilizer. All our roses, perennials with long bloom times and vegetables get a healthy dose of this rather pungent fertilizer. If gardens are weak from a prolonged lack of food, feeding with fish fertilizer is a good way to introduce micronutrients as well as a dose of nitrogen. Fish fertilizers are expensive to use on a regular basis, but they do a wonderful job in emergencies.

# COMPOST

FROM A RENOVATION GARDENING POINT OF VIEW, you cannot overstate the value of compost. It is impossible to put too much compost on impoverished garden soil. The average urban gardener simply can't get enough of this wonderful stuff.

Gardeners can make compost in backyard piles, adding organic matter layer by layer. You can produce a rich compost by combining green materials, such as grass clippings, weeds and kitchen waste, with brown materials, such as manure, straw or dead leaves, and covering the pile with a thin layer of garden soil. The smaller the pieces of material, the more quickly they will break down and the sooner the compost will be ready. Turning a pile once or twice speeds decomposition. Compost can also be made in plastic bins, rotating barrels and a number of other containers.

Free information on the specifics of composting is available almost everywhere the gardener turns, from horticultural societies and master gardening groups to municipal agencies and the cooperative extension service. Whichever approach you choose, I encourage you to make compost—it is good for both the garden and the environment.

Building your own compost pile is only one approach to getting adequate supplies of organic matter into the soil. Well-known Canadian gardener and landscape architect David Tomlinson does not apply commercial fertilizer or prepare compost for his one-acre garden, even though it contains more than 1,800 varieties of perennials. David's secret is to have his town's leaves delivered to his driveway every fall. These leaves are spread on the perennial beds as a winter mulch, and by July, there is not a leaf in sight. Worms have transformed every last one of them into rich organic matter.

Many gardens, including ours, are heavily mulched with bark chips. After a few years, some of the mulch breaks down to form a wonderful layer of organic mat-

ter just on the surface of the soil—a layer very much appreciated by the plants and microorganisms. As the bottom layer of mulch decomposes, you simply add more bark chips to the top.

Spreading bark or leaf mulch are two examples of sheet composting, which is an easy way for gardeners to improve the structure and nutrient level of their soil without a great deal of work. Sheet composting is the gardener's answer to a minimum-work soil renovation technique.

# FERTILIZERS

PLANTS NEED A BROAD RANGE OF NUTRIENTS to thrive. If they receive only what are called the macronutrients—nitrogen, phosphorus and potassium—they may grow but be stunted or unproductive. Just as important as macronutrients are micronutrients, such as iron, molybdenum and zinc. A plant might require only a speck of molybdenum throughout the entire growing season, but without it, no matter how much nitrogen it receives, it simply will not flourish.

Organic fertilizers (those made from once-living materials) are often rich in micronutrients and contain some amount of macronutrients as well. Most chemical fertilizers are high in macronutrients but contain few, if any, micronutrients. It is a gardener's job to ensure that his or her plants' nutritional needs are met. So any gardener, especially when undertaking a soil renovation, must be aware of fertilizer constituents and how they affect plant growth.

## MACRONUTRIENTS

The macronutrients are often abbreviated with their chemical symbols, N for nitrogen, P for phosphorus and K for potassium. The numbers on fertilizer bags represent the percentage of each of these elements found in the fertilizer. For example, a 10-10-10 fertilizer contains 10 percent nitrogen, 10 percent phosphorus, 10 percent potassium and 70 percent inert ingredients. The formula always lists constituents in alphabetical order.

Nitrogen is the primary element necessary for leaf growth. Without it, plants cannot form chlorophyll and their leaves will take on a yellow or pale green hue. Nitrogen is also essential for the growth of sturdy stalks.

Phosphorus acts as a highway system, transferring energy within the plant. Without it, plants cannot become established or mature. A shortage of phosphorus in the early growth stages will cause a plant to be stunted, and a shortage later will reduce flower and fruit yields. A lack of phosphorus is not always as obvious as a lack of nitrogen, but one indication is a mottling or spotting and bronzing of a plant's leaves.

Potassium is used throughout the plant in the manufacture of sugars and in cell division. Plants need sugars to fruit and flower, so a lack of potassium will reduce productivity. A yellowing on the edges of older leaves is the first symptom of a potassium deficiency; this is followed by a curling and browning of the leaf.

In general, nitrogen is needed for leaf growth, phosphorus for root growth and plant maturation, and potassium for overall plant health, fruiting and flowering. To keep any plant growing and thriving, all three nutrients are needed.

These three elements are the primary active constituents in most chemical and some organic fertilizers, but another excellent source is compost. If applied regularly and adequately for several years, compost can completely meet the macronutrient needs of garden plants. Once these critical nutrients have built up in your garden soil, they can be drawn on by the plants as we would draw on a well-stocked bank account. However, as with a bank account, if you stop making deposits, it won't be long before you can no longer make withdrawals, so compost should be routinely and generously applied.

## MICRONUTRIENTS

Micronutrients, such as iron, magnesium, manganese, molybdenum, copper, zinc and boron, all contribute some essential qualities to plant growth. For instance, if tomatoes lack magnesium, they may become bushy but they may not fruit. Some gardeners put Epsom salts around their tomatoes because it is rich in magnesium.

Without the presence of small quantities of iron, many plants cannot extract nutrients from the soil. Oak trees seem particularly sensitive to a lack of iron, and one of the indications of this absence is very light green leaves. An iron deficiency can be simply corrected: Put a handful of rusty nails in a bucket of water and wait a few days until the water turns red. Pour the water over the roots of the oak or other plant, and the foliage color should deepen within a few weeks.

In some soils, micronutrients are present but the plants cannot utilize them. The nutrients are "locked up" because the soil pH is too high or too low. Enzymes in organic matter help free up these micronutrients. Adding generous quantities of compost will moderate the pH of a soil and help plant roots absorb micronutrients. If you do not have a ready supply of compost, try adding bags of composted manure from a garden center. Seaweed fertilizers are also a rich source of micronutrients. Applied as a foliar spray or a tea, they will perk up flagging plants.

Almost all vegetables and fruiting plants benefit from a midseason application of compost, manure tea or a fish emulsion fertilizer. Roses and other heavily flowering plants benefit from weekly feedings all season. Bone and blood meal are also important supplements, but for a main course, compost is the most nutritious dish. Older plants enjoy it as much as newly established ones. If your supply is limited and you must choose between applying compost to your older or younger plants, give it to the younger ones. Then, set about to rectify the shortage by building a bigger compost pile.

# CHAPTER ELEVEN

# MAINTENANCE

*"A little neglect may breed mischief"*

BENJAMIN FRANKLIN (1706-1790)
*Poor Richard's Almanack*

WEEDS AND INSECTS CAN BE THE BANE OF a gardener's existence. Watching grass invade a perennial bed or seeing your roses reduced to lacework by Japanese beetles can weaken even the firmest horticultural resolve. In essence, much of gardening is maintenance. It is a task of providing on-going care to the plants and the soil from which they grow. When you compost, you are maintaining the tilth and organic content of the ground. When you prune a dead limb or divide a perennial border, you are maintaining the vigor of your plants.

Often, maintenance is simple and repetitive. It may involve no more than pulling weeds from your strawberry patch or picking Japanese beetles off the petals of a rose. The key, of course, to such custodial care is vigilance. A few minutes each day is more beneficial than a few hours once or twice a month. Admittedly, such vigilance is easier to talk about than to do. However, there are a number of gardening techniques that can advance your maintenance plans, even in your absence.

*Even rigorous standards of order are not difficult to maintain if you can devote a little time to the garden each day.*

# WEED CONTROL

## MULCH

Mulch is the single most important tool in the campaign against weeds. Research, funded by the Ministry of Agriculture here in Ontario, Canada, found that 4 inches of mulch eliminates 93 percent of all weeds. Although it is possible to argue against government research of this kind (any gardener could have predicted the findings), it is not possible to argue with the results. Mulch reduces weeds and that reduces work, which makes me particularly fond of mulch.

I am a lazy gardener. I much prefer to wander in the garden, enjoying the scents and colors of the flowers, than to have my knees firmly planted in the soil and my head looking down at weeds. With more than an acre of intensively planted flower beds to maintain, I have no time to play games with weeds, so I am a mulch fan. And unless you prefer weeding to smelling flowers, mulch should be an ever-present part of your garden too. Our front formal beds are covered with pine bark mulch, the perennials with cedar bark and leaves, the rock gardens with pea gravel and the nursery and vegetable gardens with straw. Mulch it or mow it is my philosophy.

Weed prevention is mulch's most important role, but it also helps to retain soil moisture. Shallow beds and sandy soils need to be watered almost daily if they are not mulched. Mulch benefits both soils and plants: as mulch decomposes, it enriches the soil with organic matter which, in turn, helps the plants. Keep in mind, however, that mulch also prevents many perennials from self-seeding, so you may want to pull away mulch from certain plants to allow some seeds to germinate.

Dozens of materials can serve as mulch, as long as they are easy to apply, will stay in place and are free of weed seeds. One material that is often promoted as a mulch but which should not be used is peat moss; it can form an impermeable crust on the soil, which will keep water from reaching plant roots. The material you choose for a mulch should depend in part on aesthetics and in part on what is locally and cheaply available. When you use local materials, your garden will reflect your own geography and be more connected to its surroundings than a garden dependent on imported materials.

We use pea gravel as a mulch on many of our personal (as opposed to commercial) gardens—on our rock gardens, evergreen collection and front formal pathways. Its gray tones show off the plants to advantage, and its texture allows the alpine seedlings to thrive and gives off a satisfactory crunch underfoot as we walk our paths.

The rarest of alpine plants thrive in a stone mulch. Carnations and other plants that have foliage that survives the winter also do well in a stone mulch because their leaves are kept dry, away from the rotting influence of wet soil. The crowns of plants like columbine also remain dry and free of rot. However, columbine and other plants that heavily self-sow will quickly become invasive on a stone mulch—the stones create conditions of optimum humidity and temperature for germination. Seedlings will have to be constantly thinned so that other plants can share the space.

Rock gardens look particularly attractive mulched with local stone. The size of the stone depends on what is available, but washed pea gravel is a good choice because it is uniform, easy to handle and resists compaction. Spread the gravel 2 inches thick over your entire rockery.

For pathways, these small round stones are more comfortable to walk on than larger stones, especially for people wearing thin-soled or evening shoes. To install a smooth and level path, water the stones thoroughly and go over them with a heavy roller. Stone pathways can be easily maintained. A good raking early in the spring and occasional light hoeing throughout the summer will keep the weeds from taking root.

Applying any type of mulch is a good fall activity.

*A thick mulch of wood chips will keep pathways neat and free of weeds.*

To begin with, prices at most garden centers are lower in the fall. Secondly, it is easier to mulch around perennials that have been cut back for the winter than it is to work among tender spring shoots. Finally, once mulched, the garden is neat and tidy and ready for the spring explosion of greenery and bloom.

## HERBICIDES

A visit to the weed-control section of a garden supply store can be a bewildering experience. The wealth of herbicides guaranteed to kill, maim or eradicate any garden problem is astounding. But the application of any of these chemicals is a two-edged sword. While they can be convenient, their use raises many environmental concerns. Much has been written about the risks and benefits of chemical herbicides, but from a gardener's perspective, perhaps the most important piece of literature is the product's label. I make a point of not remembering the formulas of the organic or inorganic sprays I use because I always want to read the label to find out the latest information about the product before using it. I am also very conscious of using a material only for its intended purpose. Herbicides are for weeds, insecticides are for insects and fungicides are for fungi.

For our own nursery and gardens at Simple Gifts Farm, we limit the use of herbicides to the chemicals and controls described below. If our intensive nursery and garden operation can prosper without the large-scale use of chemicals, there is no need for them at all in a small home garden.

Glyphosate is a nonselective herbicide; it kills what it touches. Plants absorb the chemical on their leaves and transport it to their roots, which wither and die. This process can take 8 to 14 days, depending on the size and kind of plant. Once it contacts the soil, glyphosate becomes inert, and it is supposed to break down into harmless compounds within 90 days of being applied. Glyphosate is sold under such trade names as Roundup, Clear It and Erase.

In alpine and rock gardens, where weeding can be particularly tedious, you can apply glyphosate with the "glove in glove" technique. First, put on a rubber glove (one with no holes) and then pull a cloth glove over it. Dampen the cloth glove with glyphosate and wipe your hand over the leaves of any unwanted plants. A quick swipe, enough to put a thin, visible sheen of the chemical on the leaves, is enough. This gloved technique is particularly useful for eliminating grass around clumps of such close-growing plants as hen-and-chicks (*Sempervivum* species).

There are also commercial applicators for glyphosate called weed wipers, which have a foam tip on a plastic bottle. You squeeze the bottle enough to saturate the foam, then wipe the applicator on the unwanted plants. Weed wipers eliminate the risk of herbicide drift from a sprayer.

One of our acquaintances made his own weed wiper using a hockey stick as a base. He wrapped the blade with foam and taped the herbicide container to the top of the handle. A tube runs from the container to the foam pad. He practices his slap shot on the milkweed in his fields and claims it adds interest to an otherwise boring job.

If you want to spray on an herbicide instead of applying it to plants one at a time, there is a technique you can use to protect your desirable plants. Make a spray shield from a 1-gallon plastic jug and a stick of about waist length. Cut the bottom off the jug and tape the stick to the side to make a convenient handle. Then walk around the garden, setting the jug over plants you want to save and spraying herbicide at the weeds and grass around them. Some hand-weeding may still

be necessary, but your prized plants will be spared.

Despite the fact that glyphosate breaks down into inert substances, it is a toxic material. Use safety precautions when applying it. At our nursery, we always wear rubber boots, rubber gloves, long-sleeved shirts, long pants and a spray mask when applying organic or inorganic products.

## FATTY ACIDS

A new class of herbicide has recently come onto the market that is being promoted as an organic weed killer with fast-acting, nonresidual properties. The active ingredients in these sprays are fatty acids, related to the chemicals in soaps. The acids kill plants by disrupting their cells. Usually the effects are visible within two days. Fatty-acid sprays are nonselective—they will burn wanted as well as unwanted plants. They are more effective on annual than perennial weeds; only the tops of perennial weeds are burned, allowing the roots to resprout. The herbicide quickly loses its toxicity, so you can sow seeds or set transplants into the soil within one or two days of spraying. Nevertheless these sprays can be caustic. Avoid skin or eye contact as well as inhalation.

## BOILING WATER

Boiling water poured onto perennial weeds cooks their roots quickly and thoroughly. Used against dandelions that are invading patio paving stones, the effect is immediate and convincing. Approximately 1 pint of boiling water per large dandelion root will immediately finish off the plant, if the water is poured slowly and directly on the center of the root. If applied too quickly, some of the water will run off and the plant will likely survive. Larger perennials like burdock will require more water, while small annual weeds will need less. Boiling water is nonselective; it will kill any plant and has no residual environmental impact. It is an easy way to eliminate patio weeds without hand work.

## SALT

Salt is an ancient herbicide that some contemporary gardeners have turned to for solving the problem of weeds popping up between patio stones. The ancient Romans are reputed to have used it against Carthage to eliminate the agricultural base of their rival empire. Salting poisoned the fields and kept the Carthaginians from growing food. Salt acts as a soil sterilizer. Most common weeds, as well as most desirable plants, simply will not grow where salt is concentrated.

Salt is not the perfect herbicide, though. It requires regular replacing, as it can be washed away by heavy rains or melting snow. Regardless of how benign salt seems to be, it does pollute and it does not readily break down in the food chain. Washing it away from one area in the spring simply means it will be transported somewhere else. The advantage of salt as an herbicide is that it will not hurt humans or animals.

Compared with boiling water, salt is less immediately effective but it has a longer residual impact, so it can prevent seeds from becoming established for several weeks. Nevertheless, unlike more toxic substances, it has to be reapplied several times during the summer to keep a paved patio weed-free. As an alternative to ongoing weed control, try planting an attractive ground cover between your patio stones. Once it becomes thickly established, the ground cover will keep undesirable plants from getting a roothold.

# INSECTICIDES

## SOAPS

Soap sprays are the darling of the modern garden. They have no residual effect, so they will not harm beneficial insects that were not touched by the initial spray, yet they will kill a wide range of plant-damaging creatures in their larval, nymphal and mature stages. They are most effective against nonflying or slow-flying pests, which cannot escape the spray. The soaps are composed of fatty acid salts, which disrupt an insect's normal cell membranes and cell physiology, causing cell walls to rupture and vital fluids to be lost.

A little-known fact is that soap sprays may burn some plants. Carefully test ferns, sweet peas and impatiens before spraying them. Apply soap to a small section of a plant, then wait 24 hours for signs of damage. If the plant appears unaffected, spray it entirely, including the underside of each leaf.

Soap sprays can cause eye and skin irritation. When applying them, wear pants and a long-sleeved shirt as well as a respirator. Once and only once, I neglected to wear my breathing mask. I thought about it, but it was in another greenhouse and it was cold outside. Because I apply soap sprays under high pressure to force the particles under all the leaves, the spray cloud can be dense. After spraying and breathing the mist for only a short time, I had congestion and "cold" symptoms for more than a week until my lungs recovered. While high-pressure spraying is not common in the home garden, I mention this to emphasize the importance of safety equipment for all sprays, whether of "organic" or "chemical" parentage.

## BIOLOGICALS

Buying insects to combat pests in the garden is not a new phenomenon. For years, gardeners have been ordering quantities of ladybugs and releasing them in hopes that they would eat aphids. But often, the majority of ladybugs fly into neighboring yards. With a balanced soil-feeding program and a bit of patience, most predators will come along free of charge when needed. We use a bit of soap or rotenone on aphids if these pests get too heavy and Bt (*Bacillus thuringiensis*) on cabbageworms or caterpillars, but for the most part, pests and predators are left to achieve their own natural balance.

We have only purchased one type of predator for release into the garden—the nematode *Steinernema carpocapsae*, sold under the trade name Bio-safe. This tiny creature attacks a variety of lawn grubs, cutworms, flea beetles, fungus gnats and fleas. Easy to use and effective if applied at the proper time, these nematodes do a fine job of cleaning up pests in our front lawns and garden.

## ROTENONE

Rotenone is an organic insecticide produced from the roots of certain tropical plants of the *Lonchocarpus* and *Derris* genuses, such as barbasco, cubé and timbo. It is nonselective and will poison almost any insect that ingests it—good guys as well as bad. Rotenone is particularly toxic to fish, birds and pigs, but it is relatively nontoxic to humans. Nevertheless, we wear face masks and rubber gloves when applying this powder.

One advantage of rotenone is that it breaks down in sunlight and loses its toxicity in a matter of several days, thus minimizing its environmental impact. Some formulations are mixed with water and sprayed; others are applied as powder. As with any insecticide, follow the directions on the label. Because of the short life-span of rotenone, applications can be repeated every seven days or until the problem is under control.

## BT

In our gardens, Bt (*Bacillus thuringiensis*) is one of those made-in-heaven problem solvers. It is a bacterium that paralyzes the digestive systems of specific target pests and kills them without harming other creatures, including humans. (Unfortunately, Bt is no longer marketed in Canada. The manufacturers decided that sales from the product were not large enough to justify the cost of the testing needed to meet current government registration requirements.) Bt has several different strains that act on different insects: *kurstaki* targets loopers, cabbageworms and caterpillars.

Broccoli free of cabbageworms becomes a wonderful culinary experience again instead of a minefield of tiny green surprises. The various strains of this bacterium do not hurt earthworms, birds, fish or any mammal, including humans. They also do not harm beneficial insects (other than robbing them of a food source) and can be used on vegetables right up until the day of harvest. Strains of Bt exist to control Colorado potato beetle as well as mosquitoes, blackflies and fungus gnats. Bt comes in either a powder for dusting or a liquid that is diluted with water and applied as a spray. Bt will stay active for approximately 10 days or until it has been washed off by dew or rain. Repeat sprays according to the label directions.

One curious characteristic of Bt that many beginning gardeners do not understand is that it does not directly and immediately kill the target pest. While many compounds cause insects to suddenly curl up and die, Bt forces them to stop eating. Many of the pests simply crawl off the plant but do not die for a few days. Make sure your plants are thoroughly covered with Bt, then relax—it will work.

## DORMANT AND SUMMER OIL SPRAYS

Sprays made from petroleum or vegetable oil are a growing part of the modern pest-control arsenal. Those called dormant oils are heavier and less refined than summer oils. Dormant oils are well suited to smothering insects and egg masses that overwinter on trees and shrubs. They must be applied in the spring before the buds begin to swell (hence, the term "dormant")—ideally on a day when the air temperature is above freezing so the water can evaporate, leaving the oil to smother pests.

Dormant oils can damage plants such as Japanese

*Local materials, such as stone from nearby fields, connect your landscape to its natural surroundings.*

*The harmony of the garden with the larger enviroment is best preserved by avoiding potent weed and insect killers.*

maple and can cause blue spruce to lose its blue coloring. They can affect other plants in different but equally negative ways. So before spraying a plant, make sure it is listed on the dormant oil label or test the oil on a small area of the plant and check its effects a few days later.

Summer oils, sometimes called sun oils, are lighter, more refined and appropriate for controlling insects like aphids, spider mites, scale bugs and mealy bugs on plants that are in full leaf. But, as with dormant oils, it is prudent to spray a few leaves and inspect for damage after two or three days before covering a plant entirely. A summer oil spray using vegetable oil can be concocted with the following recipe: Combine 1 cup of vegetable oil with 1 tablespoon of liquid soap, which helps the oil mix with water. Add this combination to warm water at a ratio of 2½ teaspoons to 1 cup of wa-

ter. Before applying the mixture on target insects, shake it vigorously to blend the water and oil. As with other sprays, test this mixture on a few leaves of the plant before applying it liberally.

## TANGLEFOOT

Tanglefoot is a glue that does not readily dry. It can be used in the garden as both a barrier and a trap. To keep pests like ants out of trees, wrap a 2- to 3-inch-wide strip of masking tape around the trunk. On rough-barked trees, jam bits of paper or cotton batting into the crevices to ensure a smooth fit between the bark and the tape. Holes are highways for insects to bypass the barrier. Once the tape is in place, slather it with a continuous 1-inch band of Tanglefoot. The sticky barrier keeps the insects from crossing. We have found that putting Tanglefoot directly on the trunk can soften the bark of some young trees, which is why the masking tape is advisable. In three years, when the Tanglefoot finally dries out, you can easily peel off the tape and put on a new piece. If the surface of the Tanglefoot dries out before then, rub it with a stick to expose the gooey material underneath.

As a trap, Tanglefoot is particularly effective in gardens, greenhouses and apple trees. Coat a large red ball with Tanglefoot and hang it in an apple tree; all types of pests will be attracted to the "ripe" apple and will fly over to inspect. Once they land, they will not be able to take off again. This is an easy way to trap apple maggot flies and other pests. Traps hung in the vegetable garden should be a bright lemon yellow color to attract the maximum number of flying pests (mostly aphids and whiteflies). There is some research that suggests that light blue traps work well on flower pests such as thrips. A little experimentation may be in order. While these traps can be reused, they are usually so insect-covered it is better to start fresh every spring.

# FUNGAL PROBLEMS

THE EASIEST WAY TO AVOID FUNGAL PROBLEMS is to practice good garden sanitation. This can be achieved by removing fungi's food and shelter. Following these guidelines will help keep the garden fungus-free:

• Use only healthy bulbs, seedlings, cuttings and plants to establish your garden. A diseased plant, even at a bargain price, is too expensive.

• Remove diseased plants and cuttings from the garden and burn them or put them in the trash. Do not put them on the compost pile.

• Rotate vegetable and flower crops whenever possible. Never grow the same vegetable in the same place in the garden two years in a row. Any disease left from the previous season could infect the new crop.

• Never tramp from an infected garden directly into another garden as you may be carrying infected mud or spores on your boots or clothing.

## FUNGICIDES

When all else fails and fungus or mildew attacks your plants, the sensible gardener will fight back. Lime sulfur is a useful spray. It can be purchased as a liquid from a garden center or mixed at home. In either case, it should be applied weekly or after every rain to prevent fungus and mildew from becoming reestablished.

An old-fashioned but still useful lime-sulfur spray is called Bordeaux mixture. It can be prepared by dissolving 4 ounces of copper sulfate crystals in 1 gallon of water. Then, in a separate container, dissolve 2 ounces of hydrated lime in 2 gallons of water. Add the copper sulfate solution to the hydrated lime solution to make 3 gallons of a gelatinlike precipitate.

When sprayed on plants, Bordeaux mixture sticks to the leaves and forms a protective coating. Fungus or mildew agents cannot establish themselves where the coating is thorough, fresh and active. The secret to Bordeaux mix is to use a fresh batch every time you spray. If you allow the mix to sit for a few days, the adhesive properties will be lost and coverage will be poor. Without good coverage, the spray is ineffective. But before making a broad application, test the mix on a few leaves as lime can burn many tender plants.

Baking soda can be used to make another reasonably effective fungicide. Mix between 1 and 2 teaspoons of baking soda with 1 gallon of water and apply this to plants suffering from black spot or powdery mildew. It is difficult to be precise about the amount of baking soda to use because its effectiveness is influenced by the acidity or alkalinity of the water. Be restrained in your first batch. Too much baking soda will burn tender leaves, too little will be ineffective. Experiment until you find the proper amount for your water and your plants.

# RESOURCES

*"Borrowers of books—those mutilators of collections, spoilers
of the symmetry of shelves, and creators of odd volumes.*

C. LAMB (1775-1834)
*The Two Races of Men*

I LOVE GOOD BOOKS, and I must confess to borrowing them often from my library. I also admit to a passion for buying, owning and seeing them lined up on my bookshelves and, of course, reading them. On many a winter's night, my wife, Andrea, and I tuck into bed early to escape the chill of our stone farmhouse and to explore the pages of garden literature, where we can find a land of eternal spring. Some of the books I often turn to are listed below. I hope they are as helpful to you as they are to me.

### General

*The Secret Garden.* Frances Hodgson Burnett. Boston: David R. Godine Publisher Inc., 1987. A wonderful tale of restoring an overgrown garden, with magical results for both gardeners and plants.

*The Hillier Manual of Trees and Shrubs.* Hillier Nurseries. Wiltshire, U.K.: Redwood Press, 1992. A list of plants and cultivars with brief descriptions.

*The New Royal Horticultural Society Dictionary of Gardening.* Edited by Anthony Huxley. London, U.K.: MacMillan Press, 1992. A comprehensive source on horticultural subjects. Very expensive but worth it for the gardening fanatic. These four volumes are the most used books on my shelves.

*Manual of Woody Landscape Plants.* Michael Dirr. Champaign, Ill.: Stipes Publishing, 1983. The nurseryman's essential text on plants.

*Hortus Third.* L.H. Bailey (revised by the staff at Liberty Hyde Bailey Hortorium). New York: MacMillan Publishing, 1976. This is a dictionary of plants grown in the U.S. and Canada. After the *Royal Horticultural Society Dictionary*, this is the best book on my shelf for plant descriptions.

### Pruning

*The Complete Guide to Pruning and Training Plants.* David Joyce and Christopher Brickell. New York: Simon and Schuster, 1992. Christopher Brickell is a British plantsman who really knows how to prune plants. A good basic book.

*Simon and Schuster's Step-by-Step Encyclopedia of Practical Gardening.* Edited by Christopher Brickell. New York: Simon and Schuster, 1980.

*Pruning.* Christopher Brickell. New York: Fireside Books, 1988.

*The Complete Guide to Landscape Design, Renovation, and Maintenance.* Cass Turnbull. Crozet, Va.: Betterway Publications, 1991. A basic book with a little bit of everything.

### Landscape Design

*All About Landscaping.* Edited by Cedric Crocker. Chevron Chemical Co.: Ortho Books, 1988. Good pictures and good basic ideas.

*A Guide to Estimating Landscape Costs.* Edited by Gary O. Robinette. New York: Van Nostrand Reinhold Co., 1983. For the serious estimator.

*The Small Garden.* John Brookes. London, U.K.: Marshall Cavendish Books, 1991. Just about any book by John Brookes is a feast for the eye and the imagination when it comes to garden design.

### Vegetable Gardening

*Harrowsmith Country Life Book of Garden Secrets.* Dorothy Hinshaw Patent and Diane E. Bilderback. Charlotte, Vt.: Camden House Publishing, 1991. A great book that keeps me coming back.

### Plant Care

*Organic Plant Protection.* Edited by Roger B. Yepsen, Jr. Emmaus, Pa.: Rodale Press Inc., 1976. A very useful reference on general pest control.

*Guide to Composting.* J. Minnich, J. Hunt and M. Hunt. Emmaus, Pa.: Rodale Press Inc., 1979. Explains in detail an essentially simple process.

*Diseases and Pests of Ornamental Plants*, Fifth Edition. Pascal Pirone. New York: John Wiley and Sons, 1978. A highly recommended basic reference text on plant pests and disease. It concentrates perhaps too much on chemical cures.

### Perennials

*Perennial Garden Plants.* Graham Stuart Thomas. London, U.K.: J.M. Dent and Sons, 1982. A classic. Some plants discussed are not available or will not grow in colder parts of North America. Worth reading for the prose and opinions.

*Herbaceous Perennial Plants.* Allan M. Armitage. Athens, Ga.: Varsity Press, 1989. A good descriptive book of various cultivars of perennials and, more importantly, how to tell them apart.

*Seed Germination Theory and Practice.* Dr. N. Deno, 139 Lenor Dr., State College, Pa. 16801, 1993. A self-published book that is unquestionably the best book on seed germination I know of. If you germinate perennial seeds, this book will change the way you garden.

### Trees

*A New Tree Biology Dictionary.* Dr. A. Shigo, Box 779, Durham, N.H. 03824, 1986. Self-published and available from the above address. While Dr. Shigo has authored other books, this is the best of the series for the home gardener.

*Conifers.* D.M. van Gelderen and J.R.P. van Hoey Smith. Portland, Or.: Timber Press, 1988. A wonderful picture book of evergreens, including many dwarf varieties.

### Rock Gardening

*Rock Gardening.* H. Lincoln Foster. Oregon: Timber Press, 1982. The best beginner book on the subject. If you need more information, join the North American Rock Garden Society, c/o Jacques Mommens, Box 67, Millwood, NY 10546.

# INDEX